HEAVEN ON EARTH
JESUS AT THE CENTER
OF YOUR JOURNEY TO MARRIAGE

by

ANDRAE B. RICKETTS

&

LYSBETH RICKETTS

All Photography Done By James & Lisa Hippolyte of Lyte Photography. All Rights Reserved

Copyright : 2016 by ALTTR INC. All rights reserved worldwide.

Unless otherwise noted, all Scripture references are from the King James Version (KJV).
1972, 1973, 1975, 1977, 1995 by The Lockman Scripture

Andrae B. Ricketts, ALTTR INC., Jamaica, New York, 11422, USA; Phone (662) 608-405 7; e-mail: alttrinc@gmail.com; Website: www.alttrinc.com

All Photography Done By James & Lisa Hippolyte of Lyte Photography. All Rights Reserved

We dedicate this book to two awesome married couples, Aleksandar & Miriam Popovski as well as James & Lisa Hippolyte. You guys have shown us what a marriage with Christ at the center looks like. Your marriage in and of itself is a ministry, exactly what God intended for marriage to be. You have blessed us in ways that you could not imagine. God bless you as you continue to walk with Christ on our marital journey.

Contents

1 | *Missing Preparation*   1

2 | *Learn From His Example*   14

3 | *Object Lesson #1 Drawn To Jesus*   27

4 | *Object Lesson #2 Fill My Cup Lord*   36

5 | *Object Lesson #3 In The Courtyard*   46

6 | *Object Lesson #4 No Greater Proposal Than This*   57

7 | *Object Lesson #5 Prepping For A New Life*   63

8 | *Object Lesson #8 The Day*   79

Preface

ONE of the most difficult experiences in the life of a young man or woman is when they choose a mate. God placed the desire for companionship in man starting with Adam. He recognizes our need for companionship as He tells us, "It is not good that man should be alone." (Genesis 2:18)

Yes, there are exceptions to this rule. There are those God called to forgo marriage in order to fulfill a certain purpose, such as Jeremiah or Paul to name just two. Yet most of us, expect to find ourselves getting married at some point in our lifetime.

Marriage is so important many of us focus all our attention and energy on it. Why? It is an extremely important decision. When we get married we put another person in a position of power over our lives.

In marriage, we want to find someone we can trust with ALL our vulnerabilities. This kind of trust is difficult to grant in even the best of circumstances. Christ himself struggles daily to gain the trust of those who believed in him, let alone those who do not.

All the time and energy we spend searching, usually leads us to someone we think we can spend the rest of our lives with. We then seek out guidance on courtship and dating. Which of the two, if either, should we engage in? As Christians we want to do things the right way, God's way. So we cry out to God, but many of us struggle to hear His voice on this subject.

We may hear a few short sermons on this subject in church. Some people try going to relationship seminars. Despite this most of us still don't find the answers we are looking for. Sadly love, relationships, sex, and marriage are often considered taboo subjects, unnecessary for teaching the message of salvation.

For those diligently seeking out help, premarital counseling is available during courtship. Further help in the form of marriage counseling is available during engagement and beyond. Unfortunately, there is nothing available for that time before courtship, when we are searching for a mate.

My wife and I had these same problems. But, we sought God out, and He showed us His will for our lives. The road that we travelled was a rough one, and we picked up many scars on the way. All in all, now we can see how God used our journey for good. He blessed us with His wisdom and now we have the privilege of sharing it with others. Through this we hope to see others reach the same result we have, but without the heartache and scars.

God has shown us the generic counsel and instruction given to those searching for a mate, those in courtships, and those who are married is filled with biblical principle - but void of Christ.

This always reminds us of the spiritual issue shown to us in the Pharisees. The Pharisees focused all their attention on the Laws of God (principle), while not having a relationship with Him (void of Christ). When Christ was right before their eyes, in the flesh, they failed to build a relationship with Him because of the erroneous training they received. They focused too intensely on His laws which blinded them from seeing Him in front of them.

As we search for a mate we often fall into this same pit. The church teaches us two commandments, and nothing else, for this time in our lives: 1) DO NOT HAVE PREMARITAL SEX; 2) DO NOT BE UNEQUALLY YOKED.

We are told if we follow these two commands, God will miraculously give us the relationship we are seeking. Just like with the Pharisees Christ is ignored, and absent from the situation. The reason many find this time in their life stressful is because the Prince of Peace has been excluded.

We wrote this book so that Christ can be placed back in His rightful place, the center of searching for a mate, engaging in courtship, growing during engagement, and ultimately marriage. We are asking you to join us on a journey through each phase of relationships leading up to marriage. On this journey, we will see the object lessons Christ has set for us, teaching us of our relationship with Him.

If you aren't familiar with the term "object lesson" let us explain. The parables that Christ spoke were object lessons. He taught by telling stories that were examples. Essentially, Christ would use objects that people were acquainted with as symbols for spiritual things to imbed His teachings in their mind.

For example, Christ spoke the parable of the sower and the seed to the common folk, most of whom were farmers. Farmers knew what would happen if they planted seeds by the way side, the birds would come and eat it. Farmers knew if they planted seeds on rocky ground, the seeds would not germinate, as they would be unable to get deep enough to take root in the earth. Farmers also knew if they planted seeds in an area where there were thorns, when they sprouted the thorns would choke and rip apart the plants. Finally, the farmers knew if they planted seeds on good soil, given the proper attention, the seeds would grow to fruition.

The two objects, or symbols, used in this lesson are the seeds and the types of ground. Christ used the seeds as a symbol of the Word of God, and the soil represented the hearts of men. The seeds cast by the wayside represented the hearts of those who received Truth, but Satan persuaded them to reject it. The hearts of those represented by stony ground are those who received Truth but were overwhelmed by trials and tribulations, discouraging them from continuing to abide by the truth. The hearts represented by thorny ground represented those who received the truth, but the pride of life ripped the desire for the Word from their hearts. Finally, those whose hearts were represented by the good soil are those who received and cherished the Truth. The seeds of Truth then bore fruit in the lives of these believers.

After people heard these parables they went about their days. Whenever they saw the objects (soil, rocks, thorns, the way side, farmers farming, seeds sprouting) the words of Christ would resonate in their minds through association.

Even though He has not come out and said it plainly, God has object lessons for each stage of our relationship journey. Our everyday experiences are the objects Christ uses to symbolize His relationship with us from its inception, to its culmination in paradise.

Christ desires to be at the center of our journey to marriage, just as He desires to be at the center of our study of scripture. When we begin to look for Christ in whatever stage of the journey we are on, our eyes are opened, and our spirits are quickened.

An example is the two disciples journeying from Jerusalem (Place of Peace), to Emmaus (Hot Bath or Hot Water). These two men had just experienced severe heartbreak when their beloved leader was crucified. While walking down the seven-mile road they sorrowfully recounted the loss of Christ. This resembles many who, after experiencing the end of a relationship, only focus on or talk about the suffering and pain they are going through.

Somewhere along the way, a resurrected Christ joined them on their journey, but they did not recognize Him. Having overheard their discussion He asked them why they were talking about Christ's death in such a sorrowful manner, and why they were so broken hearted.

Still not knowing this was Christ, they responded to Him as if He was crazy, thinking only a crazy person could not understand their sorrow at the loss of their savior, whom they put all their hope into.

This is a mirror image of those who put all their hope in romantic relationships, and the hurt and pain at the loss of those relationships which consumes them. The sorrow overtakes their mind, blinding them from Christ, who is right there with them. They forget He has always been with them, as he promises "I will never leave, nor forsake thee" (Heb 13:5)

After the disciples justified their reason for despair, Christ told them how foolish and weak hearted they were. He then gave them a bible study, starting from Genesis and ending at Malachi. He showed them "in all scriptures the things concerning himself." (Luke 24:27)

The disciples previously understood the word of God in principle, but Christ was not at the center of their understanding. For this reason, Christ had to reveal Himself in every scripture in the old testament to them. Christ finished the study when they got to their destination. The two disciples were so blessed they asked Christ (still not knowing it was Him) to stay with them for the night and eat with them. Then something very beautiful happened

Christ sat down to eat with them, "he took bread, and blessed it, and brake, and gave to them. And their eyes were opened, and they knew him; and he vanished out of their sight." (Luke 24:30-31)

At that very moment they jumped up and ran back to Jerusalem, excited to tell everyone what they learned. They left a place of hot water and went back to a place of joy and peace.

The road that many walk on the journey to marriage leads from a place of peace and ends at a place of scalding hot water. The worries of loneliness, decision making, and heartbreak blind them from seeing that Christ is not just taking this road with them, but has always been with them.

Christ wants us to recognize Him on our journey from singleness to marriage. That can only happen when we study this subject in the Word of God, with Christ as the center of every scripture we look at.

Bread is used in scripture to represent the Word of God, and eating bread represents a study of Scripture. When we study

Scripture, seeking Christ in everything we read, He blesses our study (blesses bread), and gives us understanding (breaks bread with us).

This is exactly what Jesus Christ did for my wife and me, which opened our eyes to His Will for our lives in this regard. We made our way from a place of scalding hot water back to a place of peace. We now desire to share our journey so others can experience the same peace, hopefully without the hot water. We would like to take you on a journey of learning Christ's object lesson on Searching, Courtship, Engagement and Marriage. We pray that the Holy Spirit turns the soil of your heart, preparing it to receive and nourish the seeds Christ provided us to sew in you. May you bear MUCH FRUIT!!!!!!!!

1 | Missing Preparation

If you are past this stage in life, please take heed. Pass this information to the generation coming after you. Also, if you desire to be a parent, this is important for your future.

We all know the proverb "Train up a child in the way he should go: and when he is old, he will not depart from it." (Proverbs 22:6) We rarely consider it, but this training prepares children for marriage and family life.

In previous generations this proverb was followed to the letter. In modern times, not as much. Parents are consumed with sustaining their quality of life and the life of their family. They do not have time to raise their children as previous generations did. Gone are the days where the father maintained the household on one salary, allowing the mother time to stay home, fully dedicated to the development of the children. Now both parents work long hours, barely making enough to pay the bills. When the parents get off work, they make sure the children eat, do their homework, take their bath, brush their teeth, and go to bed on time. They then clean the house, leaving little time to unwind from the grueling day.

Just like the object lesson of the seed planted in thorny ground, the responsibilities and cares of this world choke the Word of God, especially pertaining to training up children, out of the hearts of parents. Parents today are so overwhelmed that they allow technological devices to raise their kids. Often when little children start getting rambunctious, we see parents giving them electronic devices to play with, allowing said devices to captivate the minds of the children, keeping them still.

Something must be sacrificed in order for parents to get a moment of peace. Often the something sacrificed is Christ (no pun intended). Parents today have removed child rearing and family worship from their daily duties, using the time to catch up on their favorite shows or to have a relaxing moment. The television and other electronics are used to captivate the time and attention of children instead of interactions with parents. This is essentially, parents handing over the duties of raising their children to devices.

We have done relationship presentations in many churches where we ask young people if they have/had family worship in their home. In each of these churches less than twenty percent respond with a yes.

All the training children need to prepare them for marriage is being over looked. It is here the first principle of child rearing is missed. During family worship time, parents are to teach their children to seek "first the kingdom of God, and his righteousness." (Matt 6:33) It is in those moments when children learn to remember their creator, in the days of their youth "while the evil days come not, nor the years draw night, when though shalt say, I have no pleasure in them." (Ecc 12:1)

Parents are to set the example by seeking the kingdom of God first. Putting spiritual things before all earthly responsibilities. When they instead place their faith in the sustenance that comes from money, over God, the spiritual foundation of the family is destroyed.

The responsibility parents have in child rearing is one God takes very seriously. Consider the thought that God put into the rearing of Christ. Do you think God the Father could have given just any two people the awesome responsibility of raising the Savior of all mankind? God the Father diligently sought out a husband and wife with a character which mirrored His own. God knew that He could trust Joseph and Mary to train Christ in the way He should go. We know this because the angel of the Lord told Mary, "thou hast found favor with God. And, behold, thou shalt conceive in thy womb, and bring forth a son, and shall call his name JESUS" Luke 1:30-31.

Parents must not only prepare a spiritual foundation for their children to stand upon, they must help their children find their purpose in life. As the children recognize their purpose, the parents work diligently with them, preparing them to fulfill their purpose.

Many children grow into adult hood not knowing their purpose, or even what they want to do with their life. Stuck in this immature state is where most of us begin our quest for a mate. We ask God to provide someone who is specially prepared for us, but we are not yet mentally, emotionally, physically, financially, or spiritually prepared for such a responsibility.

We can look at the early years of Christ and see His parents ensured He received proper spiritual and mental training. We see how Christ carried these lessons into His adult years while reading Luke, chapter two.

Joseph, Mary, and a twelve-year-old Jesus went to Jerusalem for Passover. When the feast was over they started on their journey back home. Though Christ was not near them, they assumed He was in the company of travelers that accompanied them. They soon realized they were wrong. It became horrendously apparent they had left their son back in Jerusalem. After searching for three days, they found Jesus "in the temple sitting in the midst of the doctors, both hearing them, and asking them questions." (Luke 2:46)

Here is an example of the biblical training given to Christ at an early age: "all that heard him were astonished at his understanding and answers." (Luke 2:47) At twelve years old, Christ held His own against the educated men in the temple.

There was nothing different about Christ than other children. This shows our own children can, and should, have a deep understanding of the Word of God. This kind of training will serve them well throughout their lives.

When Joseph and Mary confronted Jesus, asking why He did not stay close to their company of travelers, He responded by saying, "How is it that ye sought me? Wist not that I must be about my Father's business?" (Luke 2:49) This shows Jesus knew, at the age of twelve, His purpose in life. He had a set destination He was working towards. He was not going through His adolescent years oblivious to what He was to make of himself.

His parents helped guide him to figuring out His life's purpose. As He developed into manhood, each step that He took was a step towards fulfilling this purpose. Looking more closely at the example of Christ we find that everyone has a purpose, both a spiritual and an earthly one.

Christ's spiritual purpose was manifested to us through the Word of God. Paul tells us that the mystery of Christ is, "Christ in you, the hope of glory." (Col 1:26) This means the purpose of Christ is that "in the dispensation of the fullness of times, he might gather together in one all things in Christ both which are in heaven, and which are in earth; even in him." (Eph 1:10)

Christ's objective is to be one with us. It is to gather heaven and earth as one in Him. This is the same kind of oneness a husband and wife are to experience with each other. "Therefore shall a man leave his father and his mother, and shall cleave unto his wife: and they shall be one flesh." (Genesis 2:24)

Does this mean that Jesus Christ plans to be married at some point? The answer to this question is YES! In his vision of the second coming of Jesus Christ, John is shown the uniting of the church, or believers in God, with the savior. The scene is presented as a marriage between Christ and His Church. "Let us be glad and rejoice, and give honour to him: for the marriage of the Lamb is come, and his wife hath made herself ready." (Revelation 19:7) This shows us, from His youth Christ was preparing for His own wedding.

But, let us not get ahead of ourselves. We will visit this subject throughout the coming chapters. Instead, let us place our focus back on the spiritual purpose of Christ. In His youth, He realized that His spiritual life's purpose was the salvation of the souls of mankind through Himself.

In this regard there is no difference between Christ and us. We too have both a spiritual and an earthly purpose. God has a purpose for all of us, and His desire is for us to learn our purpose during our early years. This can be proven through the life of the Prophet Jeremiah.

The Prophet Jeremiah came from a family of prophets in a very spiritual community. He was given extensive training in the ways of God. He had great mentors as examples in life. In his youth, God called him to his life purpose as a Prophet.

We know that Jeremiah was young because when God called him to be a Prophet his response was, "I cannot speak: for I am a child." (Jeremiah 1:6) God created Jeremiah, ordaining him before he was even born, for this very purpose. A purpose he was called to even though he was still young. God told Jeremiah "Before I formed thee in the belly I knew thee; and before thou camest forth out of the womb I sanctified thee, and I ordained thee a prophet unto the nations." (Jeremiah 1:5)

We would like you, the reader, to know that you too have been ordained. Before your parents ever thought of conceiving you, God ordained you for a special purpose. Your parents are to help you come to understand this purpose in your adolescent years. From then on you are to work towards it.

Every person who is single has a spiritual purpose they are expected to fulfill. Our purpose is to "shew forth the praise of him who hath called you out of darkness into his marvelous light." (1Pet 2:9) Parents are to train their children, so when they come of age, they will be equipped to share the Gospel of Jesus Christ. Children should be readily able to speak of their redeemer who has saved them from the darkness of sin and covered them in the light of His righteousness.

This is the work God expects all single individuals to engage in. This is one of the main reasons why God gives us a time period of singleness. The time we are single is when God can have our undivided attention. He can give us work to do while our hands are free from the responsibilities brought by relationships, marriage, and children.

The Apostle Paul gives the same instructions to unmarried men and women. "He that is unmarried careth for the things that belong to the Lord, how he may please the Lord: But he that is married careth for the things that are of the world, how he may please his wife. There is a difference also between a wife and a virgin. The unmarried woman careth for the things of the Lord, that she may be holy both in body and in spirit: but she that is married careth for the things of the world, how she may please her husband. And this I speak for your own profit; not that I may cast a snare upon you, but for that which is comely, and that ye may attend upon the Lord without distraction." (1 Corinthians 7:32-35)

The Word of God is instructing us to use the time we are single to prepare and build our ministries in service of the Lord. This is exactly what Christ did when He came of age. Christ took the training He received as a child and started His own ministry after being baptized by John.

If youth are trained to focus on their purpose, their hearts will not be overly consumed with romantic escapades. Yes, the longing and desire for a companion will be there. However, because their focus is entirely on Christ, He satisfies that hunger. These individuals will be able to say of God, "Thou art my portion, O LORD." (Psalm 119:57)

Satan finds those who's minds and hearts are submitted to Christ very dangerous. He sees these young people as threats, and rightfully so because the Word of God declares it.

God sees the youth in His service as "WEAPONS OF MASS DESTRUCTION" that are used to obliterate Satan's kingdom. King

Solomon was inspired to declare, "As arrows are in the hand of a mighty man; so are children of the youth. Happy is the man that hath his quiver full of them." (Psalm 127:4-5) King David tells us, God will shoot at the enemy with arrows and "suddenly shall they be wounded." (Psalm 64:7) Satan knows the best way to defend himself is to make the weapons formed against him, useless.

    The young who are not trained to keep their eyes focused on their spiritual purpose have no anchor. Without a defined purpose, they feel empty inside. They recognize a void that needs to be filled. Satan gives these wondering souls the idea money, possessions, and romantic relationships will sooth their suffering and fill the emptiness they have inside. Little do they know it is only the waters of life that can quench the thirst they have. If only they knew the only thing that can fill their soul is Jesus.

    It is here that money, possessions, and romantic relationships become an idol to which young people give all their attention, and worship. Focusing on relationships, they are initiated with the notion that the romantic connection will fulfill their life and give it purpose.

    This is where hearts are broken and lives are destroyed. No human being or material possession can take the place of God in our lives. It is impossible for God to fail us, yet Christians have a hard time understanding this. When we replace God with a romantic connection to another, we begin to expect God-like attributes from that person.

    When they fail us, and they will, it becomes too much to bear. Those who do not learn their lesson will continue going from relationship to relationship, seeking someone who can be LIKE God to them. They do not understand it is Satan, the one who desires to "be like the most High" (Isaiah 14:14), who laughs as he watches them slowly destroy themselves. This is how important training up a child is. If rightfully trained, these situations can be avoided.

    We have not yet touched on the earthly purpose given to all. This can also be seen through the life of Christ. Jesus fulfilled His earthly purpose by learning a skill and having an occupation. Again we must emphasize, this was done while He was single.

The tribe of Judah was known for producing individuals skilled in carpentry and construction. In Exodus we find the story of Uri of the tribe of Judah. The Lord filled him with the Holy Spirit, imparting to him "wisdom, in understanding, and in knowledge, and in all manner of workmanship; And to devise curious works, to work in gold, and in silver, and in brass, and in the cutting of stones, to set them, and in carving of wood, to make any manner of cunning work." (Exodus 35:31-33)

Throughout scripture we see the men of Judah overseeing construction of all kinds, especially when it came to the sanctuary of God. Christ's earthly father, Joseph, of the tribe of Judah, was also a carpenter. Joseph taught his son the craft while Christ was young. When Joseph passed away, it was Christ who sustained His home through this trade. Joseph and Jesus were both known by their occupation. When Christ began His ministry people would ask, "Is not this the carpenter's son?"(Matt 13:55) or "Is not this the Carpenter?" (Mark 6:3)

From His youth, Christ knew exactly what He was growing up to be. His mind was trained and focused on His purpose, both spiritual and earthly.

This is also the format God used for Adam's development before Eve was brought to him. God used the time Adam was single to teach him how to fulfill his purpose as manager of everything God created. "And God said, Let us make man in our image, after our likeness: and let them have dominion over the fish of the sea, and over the fowl of the air, and over the cattle, and over all the earth, and over every creeping thing that creepeth upon the earth." (Genesis 1:26)

Adam received his occupation (earthly purpose) before Eve was created. He was put "into the garden of Eden to dress it and keep it." (Genesis 2:15) We can also see the spiritual purpose of Adam fulfilled as He worked in his capacity of Manager of God's creation, through his naming of the animals. "And out of the ground the LORD God formed every beast of the field, and every fowl of the air; and bought them unto Adam to see what he would call them: and whatsoever Adam called every living creature, that was the name thereof." (Genesis 2:19)

Adam became a co-laborer with God, finishing the work of Creation. This was the ministry of Adam, all prepared and built before he obtained a wife. As a prime example, the word of God shows how Adam geared all his concentration to the fulfillment of his purpose.

After his service as a single man was completed, God then said, "it is not good that man should be alone; I will make him an help meet for him." (Genesis 2:18) God then put Adam to sleep, removed one of his ribs, and formed Eve from the rib and the dust of the ground.

When Eve was created, she did not meet Adam right away. She spent time alone with her creator just as Adam did. Eve was created not only to be a companion to Adam, but to be his "help meet" as well. Miss-understood by many, this term does not mean she was created to do chores and house work only. The Hebrew word used for help meet is ezer, and it is seen 19 times throughout the old testament. The definition of ezer shows us the role of a wife is far greater than being an individual who kisses the ground her husband walks on.

Outside the book of Genesis we see this word attributed to the Lord helping Israel fulfill their God given purpose, and helping them in their times of distress or greatest need. The word ezer means "one who helps," but it also means "to succor." To succor means to give military aid. It is Jesus Christ who provides us military aid. He is our weapon of warfare, our defense, our mighty fortress. This parallel suggests the Woman is to be like Christ to her husband.

The woman is to help her husband fulfil his God given purpose, and the word of God proves this. Speaking of Christ-like women, King

Solomon said, "A virtuous woman is a crown to her husband, but she that maketh ashamed is as rottenness to his bones." (Proverbs 12:4)

Eve was certainly the crown to her husband. It was not until after God created and presented her to Adam that God granted dominion over the earth and all the creatures in it to man. Sadly, because of the shame of sin, Eve became rottenness to Adam's bones, a saying that is not just figurative. Sin caused Adam and Eve to lose out on eternal life, instead experiencing the decay of death.

In the spiritual battle against the enemy of their souls Eve was the military help, the place of refuge for her husband. In fulfilling this purpose Eve became the final piece to Adam's installation as King of earth.

By taking the rib from Adams side to make Eve, God showed these individuals were to walk side by side as equals. This is what God initially desired the relationship to be like between a man and a wife. When sin entered the world, things changed a little bit. The curse placed on all women because of Eve's disobedience was that their husbands would rule over them. (Gen 3:17)

Many abuse this text, using it as their right to treat their wives as less than human beings. God did not say that a husband should be a dictator over his wife, the scripture means the husband will be the spiritual leader in the home.

While the man leads as the spiritual example, and provides for the family's material needs, the wife serves her husband by following his Holy Spirit inspired lead, walking side by side with him at the same time. The woman is to do whatever is humanly possible to help the man be successful in fulfilling his spiritual and earthly purpose from God.

If you believe this is old testament thinking, you may be surprised to see the new testament confirms it. "For the man is not of the woman: but the woman of the man. Neither was the man created for the woman; but the woman for the man." (1 Corinthians 11:8-9) This is a woman's purpose: she fulfills her husband, she is his crowning piece. Sadly, many women see this purpose as demeaning and lowly. This is false! The Word of God tells us that walking in this purpose makes the woman the GREATEST in the household. Jesus Christ himself lets wives know just how great they are. "But whosoever will be great among you, let him be your minister; and whosoever will be chief among you, let him be your servant: Even as the Son of man came not to be ministered unto, but to minister, and to give his life a ransom for many." (Matthew 20:2-28)

The man may be the loving leader in the home, but the wife is the chief of all in the eyes of God. She embodies the character of Christ, who got off His throne, humbled himself, and came down to earth to serve mankind.

It does not stop there. Continuing to look at this from a biblical perspective, women are not meant to stay home serving. Women have an earthly purpose of their own which God expects them to fulfill. In today's day and age women are more educated than men, and they want to put that education to good use.

Many believe the women of biblical times never worked outside of the home. It is believed that they only tended to the husband and children. The women of today do not want to be like that. We must understand, this is a misrepresentation of the word.

God never imposed any command on women to stay home, not using the talents, wisdom, knowledge, and understanding that He gifted them with. That belief is far from the truth and not supported by scripture. King Solomon tells us a virtuous wife is one who can handle her responsibilities in the home (to her husband and children) as well as using her skill and knowledge to provide financially alongside the husband. Solomon explains a virtuous wife is economically savvy and can build her own business. "She considereth a field, and buyeth it: with the fruit of her hands she planteth a vineyard." (Proverbs 31:16) In biblical times building and owning a vineyard represented building and owning a business.

Solomon goes on to inform us that a virtuous wife can create an excellent product or service for her business, and she will not go to sleep unless it is so. "She perceiveth that her merchandise is good: her candle goeth not out by night." (Proverbs 31:18) He also explains that a virtuous wife displays her business savvy by conducting business with merchants, not being swindled. "She maketh fine linen, and selleth it; and delivereth girdles unto the merchant." (Proverbs 31:2)

This looks nothing like the "common house wife" because God never intended for a wife to be common! Christ died so that men and women could not only have life, but a more abundant life.

He has great things in store for a husband and wife, but going back to the initial point, THEY MUST BE PREPARED!!!!! Have the two parties been trained from their youth in their spiritual and earthly purposes? Even if we have not been trained from our youth, we are still responsible for understanding our purposes, as the Word of God is readily available for us to study on this and many other subjects.

Instead of focusing on finding a spouse, we need to seek first the Kingdom of God and His righteousness. When we do this, all the desires of our hearts will be granted to us (as our desires will match the desires of God), that of a companion included.

God will give this to us because we sought Him out and He prepared us mentally, spiritually, physically, financially, and emotionally. Unfortunately, we usually seek the desires of our hearts before seeking the Kingdom of God. We are then unprepared for what we force ourselves into.

Also, many of us cannot hear the voice of God when we cry out to Him for a spouse. He is not speaking because we pray this prayer not to follow His will, but only to receive what we so selfishly want.

Do you see how important this preparation is? Do you see how Christ himself had to prepare for His coming marriage? Have you embarked on this journey of preparation with God?

To the young woman, you see the awesome responsibility that is before you. Surrender to God and ask Him to prepare you to walk in your purpose today. For the married woman, it is not too late. You should also do the same.

For the young man, surrender yourself to God. Ask him to focus you on your purpose in Him. Use this time you are single to serve the Lord with all the energy and attention you would not be able to give if you were in a relationship. For the married man, it is not too late for you either. Yes, it may be a bit more difficult, especially if you have children. But, take comfort and strength from knowing nothing is impossible with God. (Luke 1:27) Trust and believe that you "can do all things through Christ" who strengthens you. (Phil 4:7)

2 | *Learn From His Example*

One thing human beings cherish the most is the control we have over our destiny. Giving up this control is why so many people find it hard to become Christians. This is also why so many Christians continue to struggle with sin. The whole point of being a Christian is to surrender your will to Christ unconditionally.

Many of us struggle with surrendering our lives wholly and completely to God because we need to have a hand in the outcome of something as important to us as our future. Sometimes we may even feel God is taking too long to bring a certain result to fruition. Because of this, we believe we must get involved in order to speed up the process.

Abraham did this when he believed that if he waited any longer on the Lord to fulfill His promise of giving he and his wife a son, their already aged bodies would surely become incapable of child bearing. Today we see just how damaging their decision to bear a child with Hagar was. Out of this error comes the two groups (descendants of Ishmael and Isaac) who are presently fighting over land in Israel. This brings to life the words of Solomon, "There is a way that seemeth right unto a man, but the end thereof are the ways of death." (Proverbs 16:25)

Surrender is the hardest lesson a human being can learn, and God understands this. He is merciful and patient with us as we struggle to learn it. He understands that we have made our own plans for our lives. He also understands that it is hard to accept that what we desire the most, or how we believe we are to attain it, is not in His infinite plan for us.

Reader, if this is something that you are struggling with, we implore you to "Trust in the Lord with all thine heart; and lean not unto thine own understanding." (Prov 3:5) Pray for help in dying to yourself, allowing Christ to live out His life through you in the person of the Holy Spirit. Please do so, especially regarding this subject. Romantic relationships and marriage, when entered into apart from the Holy Spirit, can be detrimental to your health, the other person's health, and the salvation of both your souls.

God gives us a precious promise, if we do not follow our own wisdom we can be spared from this heartache and pain. "Be not wise in thine own eyes; fear he LORD, and depart from evil. It shall be health to thy navel, and marrow to thy bones." (Proverbs 3:7-8)

Many have opened their hearts to people they never should have, only to have them broken. As people who have done and experienced this ourselves, we are not condemning anyone who has fallen in this way. Rather, we would like to direct your attention to Jesus Christ who "healeth the broken in heart, and bindeth up their wounds." (Psalm 147:3) The grace of Jesus Christ is available to you. He can give you a new heart, and renew His Spirit within you.

Our mission is to direct those considering engaging in a romantic relationship to the wisdom of God's Word, so they will not have to experience this hurt and pain. We also want to show those who have experienced this hurt, the path laid out for us in the Word of God for their future benefit.

A word of wisdom from scripture to these two groups is to, "Keep thy heart with all diligence; for out of it are the issues of life." (Prov 4:23) God warns us to guard our hearts because the condition of our hearts can dictate our spiritual life. Our hearts represent our emotional state, which has a major effect on our minds. Our emotions (feelings), and our thoughts (minds) are what makes up our character. Did you know our character is the only luggage we will bring to heaven?

More than this, our character is the determining factor of whether we are saved or not. God warns us to guard our heart, because whatever enters is reflected in our personality, and shapes our character. We are instructed to keep our emotions centered on things heaven ward. "If ye then be risen with Christ, seek those things which are above where Christ sitteth on the right hand of God. Set your affection on things above, not on things on the earth." (Colossians 3:1-2)

We are instructed to keep Christ at the center of our emotions because by beholding Christ, we become changed into His "image from glory to glory." (2 Corinth 3:18) The glory of God is His character. If we behold Christ through His word (and by any other means) the Holy Spirit will shape our character into His likeness, one character change after another. Those who follow this instruction can say, "I am crucified with Christ: nevertheless I live; yet not I, But Christ liveth in me: and the life which I now live in the flesh I live by the faith of the Son of God, who loved me, and gave himself for me." (Galatians 2:20-21)

Those whose Character resembles Christ have completely surrendered to the leadership and guidance of the Holy Spirit. These are who will be called up to meet the Lord in the sky.

When we open our heart to someone that God did not intend to have the privilege, we leave ourselves unguarded from Satan's attacks. Our emotions are the number one place that Satan attacks, because they are our greatest weakness.

Because of ill-advised relationships, many of us suffer from unforgiveness, anger, and bitterness, all emotions which prevent the Holy Spirit from shaping their character in the likeness of Jesus Christ. "And grieve not the holy Spirit of God, whereby ye are sealed unto the day of redemption. Let all bitterness, and wrath, and anger, and clamour, and evil speaking, be put away from you, with all malice. And be ye kind one to another, tenderhearted, forgiving one another, even as God for Christ's sake hath forgiven you." (Ephesians 4:30-32)

If only we had a nickel for every time we have witnessed people become angry, bitter, and unforgiving because the person they trusted with their heart (whom God did not intend) broke it. Now their thoughts and feelings are centered on their hurt and pain. This in turn shapes their character into the opposite of Christ's. As they cling to these negative emotions they unconsciously resist the Holy Spirit, who cannot reside within an individual harboring such negativity. The Holy Spirit will not strive in convincing them to surrender forever. Unless they surrender their negative emotions into the hands of God, they will grieve the Holy Spirit to the point of desertion .

Just look at the example of King Saul. He was consumed by the emotions of jealousy and anger. These emotions overtook his thoughts and feelings. They caused him to fight the convictions of God, brought to him by the Holy Spirit. Sadly, he grieved the Spirit to the point that the presence of God was removed from him.

Some say this has nothing to do with love and marriage, or that dating and marriage have nothing to do with the salvation of a person's soul. Reader, if this is what YOU believe, we would like you to know you are dead wrong. The Word of God gives a perfect example through the life of Samson.

Samson was a type of Christ, meaning his characteristics and life was to resemble that of Christ. Think about it. A messenger from Heaven told his mother, who was barren, that she would miraculously give birth to a child. She was also told that her child would deliver his people from captivity. This is the same message the virgin mother of Jesus received.

This same messenger from heaven told Samson's father the same things, instructing both parents on how they were to train up this child. Just as Joseph, the father of Jesus, experienced his message of his son's miraculous birth, so too did Samson's father. After the second meeting with this messenger, who would not reveal his name, Samson's parents offered to have a meal prepared. The messenger obliged their offer. Samson's father then killed a heifer and made a burnt offering, at which the messenger went into the flames and ascended to heaven. It was then that Samson's parents realized that it was Jesus Christ who had visited them

In this we learn from God himself that training children in accordance with the purpose He has placed on them is very important to Him. There should be no leeway in this matter; strict obedience should be given to this service.

Samson was raised to be a mighty man of God, receiving his strength from the Spirit of God which dwelt in him. Delivering his people from the hands of the Philistines was his spiritual purpose. (Judges 13:5)

Samson also had an earthly purpose, to be a Judge over Israel. This meant he was well versed in the Word of God. In modern times, his position could be likened to a young person with a position in the church. Even so, Samson dealt with the same character issues that many young people deal with today. He greatly desired companionship, and he worked to attain it at any cost. He was also attracted to life outside of God, outside of the church.

Samson would often hang out in a city named Timnath, which was the land of the Philistines. It was here that Samson found his closest friends, and the woman he wanted to marry. It seems very strange that someone who was to deliver his people from the hand of the Philistines would befriend them. But, it really should not be that strange to us. Even today, Christian youth often venture into worldly associations, thinking it will have no effect on their spiritual life.

This is an area where Samson's parents failed in their child rearing. They did not properly admonish their son for walking on Satan's ground. It hurt them to not give him what he wanted because they loved him so much. They never thought that they would experience parenthood because of Samson's mother's barren womb. For an Israelite, not having a child was embarrassing, but beyond this, not having a male child to carry on the family name was shameful. Now they had a child, a son, and in that excitement their love for Samson overshadowed their obedience to God.

Their failure to properly instruct Samson allowed him to grow up doubting the God given command: do not be unequally yoked with unbelievers. (2 Cor. 6:14) As a leader he was to uphold this commandment, being an example to those around him and those that came after him.

Today we see this happening with the youth in our churches. They too, doubt this same God given command. What is their argument against it? They see others, who should be examples to them, in unequally yoked associations and romantic relationships which seem harmless. What they don't see is what happens behind closed doors. If they were able to see the arguments taking place over spiritual matters, they would think twice. If they could see the number of leaders in the church who must compromised their beliefs and their purpose to appease their counterpart, it would shape their thoughts differently.

"But there is a God in heaven that revealeth secrets" (Dan 2:28), who brought us behind closed doors into the life of Samson, showing us what is down this path. The life of Samson is THE PRIME EXAMPLE of what not to do in searching for a mate.

In Timnath, Samson saw a beautiful Philistine woman. Just by her looks he decided this was the woman he was going to marry. This emphasizes how Samson knew very little about this woman, and his attraction to her was based completely in lust. Samson confirms that his decision was based purely in lust with his response to his parents objection regarding his decision: "Get her for me; for she pleaseth me well." (Judges 14:3)

This is the same error many of us make when deciding to date someone. We know very little about the character of the individual, and only see a small portion of their personality. The biggest draw to them is physical attraction, which allows lust to control our mind. Lust causes so much heartache and pain. When lust is the foundation of our choice of a mate, it causes our ears to close off to and miss the Holy Spirit's promptings. Without the wisdom of the Holy Spirit ordering our footsteps in this situation, lust will direct our feet down the path of emotional ruin. "But every man is tempted, when he is drawn away of his own lust, and enticed. Then when lust hath conceived, it bringeth forth sin: and sin, when it is finished, bringeth forth death." (James 1:14-15)

King Solomon was also inspired to speak about lusting after the physical attributes of others. "Lust not after her beauty in thine heart; neither let her take thee with her eyelids." (Proverbs 6:25) Even though King Solomon directs his speech to men in this text, it is applicable to women as well.

Our tendency to lust is why we must allow God to lead us in the search for a mate. He chooses in a totally different way. The way that God directs us to choose a mate can be seen in how He chose David to be the next King of Israel.

God sent Samuel to the house of Jesse to find and anoint the next king. Samuel almost chose a king in the same manner that many choose a mate, looking at their physical attributes. Samuel saw that Jesse's son, Eliab, was the most handsome and strongest of all the children. Samuel said to himself "Surely the LORD's anointed is before him." (1 Samuel 16:6)

God quickly stopped Samuel from anointing Eliab exclaiming, "Look not on his countenance, or on the height of his stature; because I have refused him: for the LORD seeth not as man seeth; for man looketh on the outward appearance, but the LORD looketh on the heart." (1 Samuel 16:7)

These are the same words God is admonishing us with. In our search for a mate, do not look at his or her physical attributes, but rather at their heart, better known as their character. We must inspect and determine if they have a character resembling Christ's.

Please do not get us wrong, we are not saying physical attraction plays no part in choosing a mate. We are saying it is not the fundamental principle. By standing on the foundation of physical attraction, we are building our relationships on sinking sand. It is best that we follow the Word of God and build our relationships on a sturdy foundation, the ROCK JESUS CHRIST.

Samson continued to build his spiritual life on sinking sand, travelling to Timnath and arranging to take this young woman as his wife. During his travels, he came across a lion standing between him and Timnath. We are told that the lion roared against him, but a fearless Samson slaughtered the beast with his bare hands. This is significant because it foreshadows Samson's downfall, as the Lion represents Christ and the roar represents His prophetic word.

While speaking of this roaring lion, the Prophet Amos explains the Lord "revealeth his secret unto his servants the prophet, The lion hath roared, who shall not fear? The Lord God hath spoken, who can but prophesy?" (Amos 3:7-8)

Christ used the lion as a last attempt to get Samson thinking twice about the action he was about to take. The roar of the lion represented the voice of God, intended to bring fear to Samson, turning him from his wicked ways. The roar also represented a prophetic word, warning Samson that the path he was treading lead to his destruction. Sadly, Samson disregarded the warning of the Lord and killed the lion.

Today, the Lord gives the same warnings to His people in this situation. Often we say we cannot hear the voice of God telling us whether we should or shouldn't pursue a relationship with a certain prospect. The reality of the matter is, the Lord is roaring at us like a lion. He uses His Word, people who give wise counsel, and situations to tell us whether we should go any further. But like Samson, lust consumes our attention, so much so that we are unable to see. Similarly, it clogs our ears so we are unable to hear.

It is not God that is quiet, it is we that overlook His great warnings. It is only after we disregard His warnings that God becomes silent. Think about it, would you be interested in speaking to someone who constantly ignored you while you had something important to tell them? When we disregard the Lord's warnings, we are putting his word to death in our lives.

There is a wise proverb parents tell their children, "those who do not learn by hearing, will always learn by feeling." It is like when a parent strongly instructs a child not to touch the stove. Unfortunately, the child's fascination with the stove causes the warning to go in one ear and out the other. It is only when the child touches the stove they realize this is a thought they never should have entertained.

After Samson reached Timnath he arranged the marriage, after which he began his journey home. Using the same road to go back, Samson came across the lion he had killed. Looking at the lion, he saw a swarm of bees had produced honey inside its carcass.

Samson, who we can only suppose was severely hungry, collected some honey for himself and his parents to eat. In that day, it was unlawful for an individual to touch the body of a dead animal, much less eat from it (According to the ceremonial laws). When giving the honey to his parents, Samson did not tell them where it came from.

This represents how sweet the sins that we cherish in our lives are. We know it is wrong but we do it anyway, because it tastes so good to the flesh. West Indians have a saying that applies perfectly to this analogy, "SIN IS SWEET."

Samson knew what he did was not in accordance with the Word of God, but all that mattered to him was feeding his flesh. There are those today who know they are walking on dangerous ground regarding their romantic escapades, but they can't resist their flesh's appetite for the sweet nectar of sin.

Samson fed his appetite by marrying this woman. He celebrated by holding a feast for seven days. At the beginning of the feast Samson issued a challenge to his Philistine friends. The challenge was to solve a riddle he created. If they could not, they would have to pay him a large sum of money.

After three days of trying to figure out the riddle these so-called friends realized they would lose the challenge if they did not do something quickly. They decided to force Samson's wife to get the answer out of him, for them. They also threatened to kill her and her father if she did not comply.

Here the command of not being unequally yoked with unbelievers comes to life. Samson's wife feared the Philistines more than she trusted the Power of God dwelling within Samson. On the seventh day of the feast, before the sun went down, she tricked Samson into giving her the answer to the riddle. Then she gave it to his friends.

Samson trusted his wife with the answer to the riddle. There was an implied agreement that this was to stay between them. Yet his wife broke the covenant they had with one another. She did this before the sun set on the seventh day, which is symbolic of the Sabbath. If a lack of faith caused her to break the covenant she had with her husband, it is safe to say she would not keep the holy covenant of the Lord.

With Samson representing a type of Christ and his wife a pagan, we are sure the Apostle Paul wrote these words with Samson in mind, "And what concord hath Christ with Beliel? Or what part hath he that believeth with an infidel?" (2 Corinthians 6:14)

As believers, we have no business engaging in romantic relationships with people who do not believe in Jesus Christ, or who are not serious about their walk with Him for that matter. Samson learned a lesson that all Christians who have his lustful mindset need to understand.

Only the Holy Spirit can convict someone of the truth, and wring out conversion in their life. It is impossible for YOU to do this yourself, using a relationship beyond that of a platonic friendship.

If we decide to force the situation, we only hurt ourselves and our interests. Returning to the example of Samson, his heart was broken when his father in law took his wife and gave her to Samson's so called Philistine friend to marry.

Out of anger Samson retaliated against the Philistines, inciting them to get back at him. They killed his ex-wife and her family. Do you see the trail of destruction Samson's sin caused? He experienced a broken heart, and a young woman and her family were killed. All because of succumbing to lust.

In our case the outcome may not be as severe, but it is still painful. Anyone who has experienced a broken heart understands that it causes the inability to eat or sleep. There is a pain that cannot be soothed, and most would do anything just to feel better. Many people turn to alcohol, others turn to drugs, and some even commit suicide because they just can't bear life without that special someone. However, the most common stimulant used to ease this pain is fornication.

This is not a new trend, it is the same coping mechanism Samson used to ease the suffering of his loss. "Then went Samson to Gaza and saw there an harlot and went in into her." (Judges 16:1)

It did not take Samson long to recover and forget about the ordeal he had gone through. Soon after he saw another Philistine woman that pleased him. "And it came to pass afterward, that he loved a woman in the valley of Sorek, whose name was Delilah." (Judges 16:4)

Samson, not learning from his previous mistake, began going down the same path of destruction as before. This is no different than people today who go from one failed relationship to the next, making the same mistake over and over and over again.

The spirit of lust that was strong in Samson is strong in the Christian youth of today. They share the same eagerness Samson had to prove that unequally yoked individuals can coexist. We can testify of the many Christian Singles Relationship seminars we have been to where young people angrily defended the belief that there is nothing wrong with joining a non-believer in a relationship.

They cannot understand this command was not given to restrict them from pleasure, but rather, to save them from suffering, heartache, and pain. I can just imagine God sadly saying to himself, "There is a way that seemeth right unto a man." (Proverbs 14:10)

Just as with Samson, Satan knows that he can use lust and the idolizing of relationships to capture believers in his net. He leads believers to compromise their belief for the sake of lust, as Samson did.

He even causes believers to fall from their God given purpose. Samson, the once mighty Judge and Deliverer of Israel, was reduced to a blind sideshow attraction for the Philistines by the betrayal of Delilah in the same way.

Remember, when God brings a man and woman together, it is so they can both fulfill their purpose in Him. Ordained relationships and marriage bring glory to the name of the Lord, but when we walk in our own wisdom it dishonors God, and leaves us broken.

It is for this reason we implore you to put dating to the side, and seek the Lord. Come before Him daily, dying to your flesh. Allow the power of the Holy Spirit to impart the power of Christ to you.

Through Christ, you will gain the ability to overcome lust and silly infatuations, Satan's best weapons against the Christian youth of today. Most importantly, by beholding Christ, you will realize the promise of the Holy Spirit shaping your Character daily in the image of Christ.

You may be thinking, "This sounds good... But this is supposed to be a book geared towards Godly relationships... What gives???" Well, this is the answer to how you find your significant other.

While we surrender to God He is not only prepping us for a relationship with Him, but also to be trusted with the gift of the mate He will bring to us. That's Right!!!! We do not search for our mate, one will be provided to us by God.

Just as he did for Adam and Eve, God does the same for us. Both Adam and Eve spent personal grooming time with the Lord, building a relationship with Him before their relationship with each other started.

It was the Lord that brought the two together, neither one had to embark on a stressful and exhausting quest to find the love of their life as seen in movies. Rather, God led them to each other for the first time, in a meeting that was arranged from before their birth.
If you would like to learn how God goes about His match making, please continue reading with an open mind. If you do, we are sure you will be blessed by how the Godhead is revealed along your journey towards companionship.

3 | *Object Lesson #1*
Drawn To Jesus

We have learned Jesus Christ Himself is preparing for His wedding, a grand ceremony to be held at His second coming. Since He has made it this far in His relationship journey, it is safe to assume there was a point where He was searching for a mate.

For those at this point in life, your safest bet is to emulate what Christ Himself has done, being that He is our example. We can learn the method Christ used by applying the same technique that opened the eyes of the disciples on the road to Emmaus.

When we place Christ at the center of any story we read in the bible, we come to some amazing discoveries. Such a discovery is by found seeking Christ in the story of Isaac finding a wife. Did you know that the way Isaac found his wife is the same way that Christ finds His bride? Truer words have never been spoken, and we can prove this by a Christ centered study of Genesis Chapter 24.

Think of this story as a play with four actors, Abraham, his most trusted servant, Abraham's son Isaac, and Isaac's wife to be, Rebekah. Imagine that the title of this play is, "A Help Meet Found." Next, the actors are given their parts. Father Abraham will play, God the Father. Abraham's son Isaac will play the part of, God the Son. To make the Godhead complete, Abraham's servant will play the part of the Holy Spirit. Last but not least, Rebekah will play the part of the Church, bride of Christ.

The play opens with God the Father meeting the Holy Spirit. He informs the Holy Spirit He is looking for a wife for His Son, Jesus, and He wants the Holy Spirit to go find this woman, and bring her to Jesus.

God the Father makes the Holy Spirit swear He will choose a wife for Jesus out of His people. This promise also included a demand that the Spirit would not bring Jesus back to the land of the Father, but the Spirit will bring the Woman to Jesus. {FREEZE FRAME}

As the actors stand frozen on the stage, let us analyze this script. Since this is a true story that happened to the people we are imagining to be actors, a good question would be why have we replaced them with new characters?

In all actuality, the story found in Genesis 24 is the other way around. This is the real-life experience of God the Father, The Holy Spirit, Jesus Christ, and the Church. (Us.) Yes, we know it is a bit confusing, but please stay with us, it will become clear in a moment.

In biblical times, the head of the household shared his authority with his eldest son and lead servant. The eldest son and the lead servant could represent the father concerning various matters if need be. All three individuals shared a love for one another and easily worked as one unit. If you were to meet the son or the servant it was as if you met the father.

This is the kind of relationship that Abraham had with his most trusted servant and his son Isaac. This is the same relationship seen between God the Father, God the Son, and the Holy Spirit; the Godhead.

Various scriptures use the hand of God the Father to represent the Holy Spirit, meaning He does the work of the Father. Yet, scripture also shows that the Holy Spirit shares in His authority as Christ tells us, "him that blasphemeth against the Holy Ghost it shall not be forgiven." (Mark 12:10)

Blasphemy is something that can only be done against God. Consequently this is one text of many showing the Holy Spirit shares in God the Father's authority. Another text showing God the Father and the Holy Spirit share authority is Acts chapter 5. There Peter tells Ananias that lying to the Holy Spirit is lying to God.

Do you now have a better understanding of how the relationship between Abraham and his servant is an image of the relationship between God the Father and the Holy Spirit? What about Christ then?

Just like Samson, Isaac is a type of Christ. Isaac's life and character foreshadows that of Christ. The resemblance is seen when God asked Abraham to sacrifice his "only begotten son." (Heb 11:17) This could be confusing because we know Abraham had a son before Isaac, so how could this be his only child? The word begotten means the one most like. The understanding we get here is Isaac was the son out of the two most like his Father Abraham. Abraham was commanded to kill the son whose character was most like his.

God spared Isaac before Abraham could slay him with the dagger. The minds of the father and son were then directed to the fact: this is the sacrifice God the father is to make with His Son.

This was made clear to them when God the Father provided a lamb, in place of Isaac, which represented Jesus Christ. Mount Moriah, the place where Isaac was spared, is the same place where Christ was crucified.

The correlation is summed up in this verse, "For God so loved the world, that he gave his only begotten Son, that whosoever believeth in him should not perish, but have everlasting life." (John 3:16) Jesus Christ, the Begotten of the Father, is so much like the Father, if anyone sees Him they have "seen the Father." (Jhn 14:9)

Paul also tells us Jesus Christ shared the same authority as God since He, "Being in the form of God, thought it not robbery to be equal with God." (Phip 2:6) This is how three separate entities, with different personalities and different roles, can hold one title: God.

We pray that you are beginning to understand how God uses the real events of Genesis 24 as an allegory of Christ's introduction to His bride. Pay close attention. This is the meat of the subject.

In Isaac's day marriages were arranged by the parents, most namely the father. This is a system instituted by God, so it made sense for God the Father to follow His own methods.

Jesus does not have to look for His bride. God the Father instructs the Holy Spirit on what type of woman to bring to Him. Jesus Christ Himself tells us this is true saying, "No man can come to me except the Father which hath sent me draw him." (John 6:44)

It is God the Father who sends the Holy Spirit to draw us to Christ, just as Abraham sent his servant to draw a wife to Abraham. Similarly, God the Father does not desire for Christ to be brought back to the area the woman comes from any more than Abraham desired that for Isaac.

This is the reason why Christ's feet will not touch the earth at the second coming, but rather we will be caught up to meet Him in the air, just as Rebekah was brought to Isaac. We know your wheels must be turning right now as your eyes have been opened to the revelation of Christ in this scripture. We are sure your mind has brought you ahead of the words on this page as you apply this analogy to the rest of the story. For those who still need some help understanding, we will explain the rest.

Abraham told his servant what to look for in a woman, and what to say when she was found. The servant knew not to speak his own opinions, or do his own will. Christ tell us, when God the Father gives the Holy Spirit instructions on who to draw to the son, the Spirit "will not speak of himself; but whatsoever he shall hear, that shall he speak." (John 16:13)

While studying the example of Christ seen through the life of Isaac in finding a mate, we start to understand God's method of doing so. We do not have to search for our mate, it is not something God expects us to do. We do not have to play dating Russian

Roulette, hoping we will luckily meet the right person. God has already sent the Holy Spirit out to draw that mate to us. He did the heavy lifting for us.

It is here many of us worry God will bring a mate that is unpleasant to the eyes. God is more interested in the character of a person, but this does not mean that He will bring an individual we will not be attracted to.

This is the physical description of Rebekah: "the damsel was very fair to look upon, a virgin, neither had any man know her." (Genesis 24:16) Rebekah was very attractive, but so were the other woman before the eyes of the servant as he sat by the well in the city of Nahor.

What made Rebekah stand out is that she had the true characteristic of a help meet. The servant came to Rebekah begging for water because he was thirsty and she did not hesitate, humbling herself to give him water. Not only this, but Rebekah then began to draw water for the ten camels that the servant brought with him, of her own volition. On average a camel can drink up to thirty gallons of water, so this woman drew about 130 gallons of water from this well, all by herself.

It is obvious now why the servant chose Rebekah over all others, she had the heart of a true help meet. He was sure Rebekah would certainly do all in her power to help his Master's son fulfill his God given purpose. In this same way, God, by the Holy Spirit, searches the hearts of men, drawing who He will to Jesus Christ.

For all the single Christian men out there, this is what God is willing to do for you if you would just trust Him. The person that God finds for you is far better than the person you will find for yourself. This does not mean the one you find on your own is a bad person, they just are not who God designed to help you fulfill your purpose. Also, this does not mean you are to sit back and just wait for God to bring that special lady to you. You have a task to complete as well.

This can be seen in what Isaac was doing when Rebekah was brought to him.

"And Isaac went out to meditate in the field at the eventide: and he lifted up his eyes, and saw, and behold, the camels were coming." (Genesis 24:64) Here we see that Isaac went out to have evening worship, and to meditate on the word of the Lord. It was at this moment he met his mate.

The custom of that day was to have morning and evening worship. This shows Isaac was serious about having his own personal relationship with his heavenly Father. It shows that Isaac was one who did the will of his father. We see this same characteristic in Christ who said, "I came down from heaven, not to do mine own will, but the will of him that sent me." (John 6:38)

Dear brothers, when you self-examine your life, when you search your heart, can you say the same for yourself? Is spending time with God in worship and meditating on His word something that is the staple point of your life?

Have you purposed in your heart, like Daniel and the three Hebrew boys, that all you learn in scripture you will adhere to by the power of the Holy Spirit? If this is not so, how can you expect God to give you that special someone?

If God brings you a woman who has completely surrendered to Him while your own heart has not been rendered, you will only destroy this woman. It would not be fair to the woman for God to do so.

We are pretty sure that Rebekah wanted a God-fearing man as well. God met her desires by introducing her to Isaac while he was engaged in worshiping the Lord. God so lovingly showed her the character of Isaac before she even spoke to him, just to give her assurance that this was His doing.

{Andrae Speaking} Before I met my wife, at the age of 24, I had just gotten out of a terrible relationship which so devastated me that suicide was the only option I saw to overcome the pain. I thought that my ex was the person I would spend the rest of my life with. Suddenly I felt as if I had no purpose, no reason to live.

Even though I was born into a Christian family, I never really took my faith seriously. But in a last-ditch effort to cling to some kind of hope, I remembered the God that my mother taught me about.

I prayed this prayer, "God, I know that I have not really had a relationship with you, but if you are real and love me as you claim, please give me a purpose to my life. Take this hurt and this pain away. If you do this, I will say whatever you want me to say, I will go wherever you want me to go, and I will do whatever you want me to do. If you don't do this, then there is no real reason for me to live."

In that moment, I felt a warmth surrounding myself, as if there was someone embracing me. I also felt a cooling sensation inside of me, an incredible sense of calm, and peace overtook me. God let me know He heard my prayer by sending me the comforter, the Holy Spirit.

From that day forward I began building my relationship with God, cherishing my worship, study, and meditation times. I began to understand for myself why I am a Christian, and that I had a responsibility to share the light of Jesus Christ with all I could.

I began talking to my friends about Jesus Christ and their eyes began opening as mine had. I also received invitations from churches all over my city to encourage their youth to take their spiritual life seriously. I even became the youth leader of my church.

I now looked to God to help me overcome the hurt and pain from my past, rather than seeking salvation from another woman through a relationship. I no longer wanted to put a human being in the place that only God should have in my life.

I promised God that I would not get into another relationship until He brought me a woman that had the same mindset as myself. Don't get me wrong, I was not asking God to send me the most perfect and holiest woman of all time, but rather one that had a mind and desire to serve God.

I promised God that I would not consider pairing myself with someone unless they could help me (help meet) stand faithfully in Him, just as much as I would help her do the same. I desired a Godly woman that would not compromise herself, even for me.

Shortly after I made this vow to God, the most beautiful woman I have ever seen in my life walked into my church, the rest of which will be recorded in the coming chapters. I did not have to search for her, she was literally drawn to me.

The only explanation I can give as to how we met for the first time is the hand of God. I was totally asleep, focusing completely on my relationship with God. But God woke me up to a woman who was not only beautiful, but serious about her relationship with Him.

A chaste woman, who herself got out of a bad relationship and made a decision to focus on her ministry rather than get into another relationship. A woman who made a vow that the next relationship she got into would be one that led to marriage.

Her vow included a promise that she would wait on God to provide her a man serious about his spirituality. She specifically prayed for someone who had his own ministry, a man that could help her in her walk with Christ just as much as she could help him.

Most importantly, she wanted God to send her a man that understood her virginity was a gift from God, only to be unwrapped by the one she says "I DO" to. Reader, I can confidently tell you the Holy Spirit led Lysbeth Jean-Louis to me, just as He brought Rebekah to Isaac.

For the single men, be like Adam and Isaac who built their relationship with God before they got into, or even thought of, a relationship with another person. God was their very first romantic relationship, in which they learned how to love their wives.

For the single ladies, be like Eve before the fall. Spend your single moments with God, and as you build your relationship with Him, He will prepare you to be a help meet, a type of Christ, to your mate.

Adam was put to sleep while Eve was created. Eve knew nothing of Adam until God brought her to him. Your search for a mate should be the same. Put your focus entirely on God, and while you are unaware, when God sees fit, He will send His Spirit and draw your mate to you.

Now your question may be, when I meet my mate, what do I do next? Don't worry, God has that covered. Jesus Christ, by His example shows how this is done through the true story of "the woman at the well". If you thirst for the answer, continue reading and quench it.

4 | *Object Lesson #2*
Fill My Cup Lord

The best place to see the power of Jesus Christ displayed in the Gospel is the book of John. Matthew spoke on Christ's royal attributes, Mark revealed His role as a servant, and Luke focused on the truth of His humanity.

But it is the book of John that displays the raw, unstoppable power of God. This book is so powerful I recommend it as the starting point for new Christians as they begin to study the Bible.

It is here we see Jesus Christ in all His glory, teaching men and women who the Holy Spirit has drawn together, how a romantic relationship is to begin. No, I am not saying that Christ got into a physical relationship, but rather, each stage of a relationship is an object lesson in the Gospel.

Remember, Christ gave object lessons in the form of parables so the common person could see Him in their everyday life. The first encounter of two people who the Holy Spirit has drawn together is an object lesson of our first encounter with Jesus Christ.

For us to accurately view the object lesson, we must first gain an understanding of how a man and woman approach a romantic relationship. Not to worry! Christ, in His glory and power, teaches us this lesson through the story of the woman at the well.

John chapter 4 is where God uses the Gospel to show how a romantic relationship should form. Jesus Christ, by example, shows the role a man, and the Samaritan woman shows the role of a female. In this single divine encounter, Christ shows how two individuals, over a period of time, fall in love with each other. There is a radical difference in Christ's method and what we believe to be the norm.

The story begins in Samaria as Jesus and his disciples traveled from Judaea to Galilee. Jesus, weary from his travel, sat at Jacobs well to rest while the disciples went to the city to buy food.

We liken this to men who are tired of traveling from one relationship to the next. They are weary from the emotional exhaustion of putting all their hope and effort into a relationship, only for it to fail. Jesus is asking us to stop our castle building for a moment and to come rest at Jacobs well.

We promise, if you "rest in the Lord and wait patiently for him" (Psm 37:7) He will give you the desires of your heart. God the Father did this very thing for Christ as He drew the Samaritan woman to Jacobs Well, by means of His Spirit.

Remember, Christ Himself said no one comes to Him unless His Father draws them. It is the same for all men, God will draw the woman to you. And not just any woman, but the one He has prepared.

The Samaritan Woman was not just a random woman stopping by to draw water. God the Father specifically picked a woman who was not perfect, but had a heart yearning for a closer relationship with Him. As this woman comes to the well to draw water, Christ says to her "Give me to drink." (Jhn 4:7)

As Jesus walked down the road, he became thirsty on top of being tired. Those resting from tiresome relationship travels develop an unquenchable thirst. This thirst is from the God given desire to connect with someone. When you take a moment to rest in the Lord, to wait patiently on Him, He will bring to you the only woman who can quench your thirst. And know this, the Spirit of God will give you the wisdom to discern if this is the one, as He did for Christ in this situation.

It is in Christ making the first move, asking the Woman to draw him some water, that we learn who pursues who. The man pursues the woman, not the other way around. The man strives for the woman's attention while professing his intentions.

The man expresses his interest in the woman, letting her know he believes she can quench this thirsting of his soul. In studying the mighty men of the Old Testament, you will find they all made the first move. Why not follow this example?

Just think about how YOU fell in love with Jesus. You did not have to go out and win His affections. John tells us, "We love Him because he first loved us." (1Jhn 4:19) Jesus Christ, the man of all men, won your affections over, and He expects you to follow His example when bringing you your Rebekah.

To the ladies, you are the gift of God to man. A gift they must win over. Be patient. Wait on the Lord. He will lead you to your Isaac who will win over your affections. If you do it any other way, you take over the man's role.

Something else to consider is the recent social norm for women to chase after men, thinking the good ones are scarce. Women seeking relationships constantly approach single men. If we do the same we risk them missing what makes us special, instead being seen the same as the rest.

When we follow God's method we stand out among all others as peculiar women. (1 Pet 2:9) We will be seen as a crown (Prov 4:9) that he desires to attain and cherish. But do not get it twisted, do not fall for any kind of sweet talking man.

While the Holy Spirit promises to draw us to the right man, the enemy of our soul, Satan, loves to come disguised as an angel of light. (2 Corn 11:14) For this reason, do not be surprised if he brings someone pretending to be sent from God, but who is really his minister. (2 Corn 11:14)

We encourage all women to "believe not every spirit, but try the spirits whether they are of God: because many false prophets are gone out into the world." (1 Jhn 4:1) Trying the spirits means to test the person to see whether they are sent by God or not.

This is exactly what the woman at the well did, she tested Jesus with various questions, trying to figure out who this man was. The first questions she asked was "How is it that thou, being a Jew, askest drink of me, which am a woman of Samaria? For the Jews have no dealing with Samaritans." (John 4:9) The Samaritan woman is observing that she and Jesus are not the same kind of people. She does not see Him as compatible, or believe they could get along.

You may be approached by someone who you do not see as your type, just as the woman at the well was approached by a non-Samaritan. The truth is, what we believe to be our type may be wrong. There is a God in heaven who knows our true type, and can provide exactly what we need. Do not be too quick to think "He isn't my type." Imagine how different this story would be if the Samaritan woman cut Jesus off at this moment.

There are many women that miss the blessings of God because they have an image of the perfect man in their mind. Because of this mindset, they constantly fall for the wrong guy and they eventually succumb to the falsehood that there are no good men in the world.

Again, we are not saying to throw yourselves at every man that approaches, but to follow the method presented in the gospel and test the spirit. Determine whether they are from God or not. When we seek out God in the situation, He will show himself. Those who seek God out in any situation can claim this beautiful promise, "Ye shall seek me, and find me, when ye shall search for me with all your heart." (Jeremiah 29:13) The question to ask is, are we seeking God out in the relationship quest with all our heart?

Men, we must look at how Christ proved himself during the Samaritan woman's testing. Christ responded saying, "If thou knewest the gift of God, and who it is that saith to thee, Give me to drink; thou wouldest have asked of him, and he would have given thee living water." (John 4:10) In the same manner we are called before the Lord to humble ourselves (Jm 4:10), but are also encouraged to come before his throne of Grace boldly (Heb 4:16). Using this method, Christ humbly but very boldly informed this woman what she would be missing out on in Him, if she passed him by.

When you come face to face with the gift God has given you, be confident and speak with the same authority that caused people to pay attention to Christ when He spoke. Yet in your tone and approach, there must be a soft and humble touch.

Women are attracted to men who have confidence in themselves, confidence which is visible through a gentle and humble spirit. This allows you to get closer to her affections. Like Christ, you let your interest know there is something special about you that she should take heed of.

This may not be enough to solidify a position in the life of your interest, but it will gain her attention, and in a good way. Christ's response to the Samaritan woman did such a thing, prompting her to further investigate what manner of man Christ was.

Her next question was, "Sir, thou hast nothing to draw with, and the well is deep: from whence then hast thou that living water? Art thou greater than our father Jacob, which gave us the well, and drank thereof himself, and his children, and cattle?" (John 4:11-12)

What the Samaritan woman is saying here is, Jesus is offering her water of Himself, outside of Jacobs well. But there are so many that have come to drink from Jacobs well, even Jacob himself and his immediate children. Essentially the Samaritan woman asked Christ if He believes that He is any different or better than all others who have drawn from this well. This scripture represents those who have drawn from the relationship well many times.

We look to quench our thirst with one individual, but the relationship fails. We must draw again, and again, and again. This is something the Samaritan woman experienced. She struggled through five failed romantic relationships, and the man she was currently with, number six, was about to fail too.

Men, we may not be the first person that our interest was in a romantic relationship with. The question she may pose is, "I have been in many relationships and have heard the same thing, what makes you different from all the other guys? What is it that you have to offer that is better than those who came before you?"

This is Christ's response to that questions, "Whosoever drinketh of this water shall thirst again: But whosoever drinketh of the water that I shall give him shall never thirst; but the water that I shall give him shall be in him a well of water springing up into everlasting life." (John 4:13-14)

Christ is telling the Samaritan woman that she continuously draws from this well. She thinks one day her thirst will be quenched, but it won't. Christ alludes that all the people she has named drew from this well, yet they are no longer living.

This is also spoken to women who continuously draw from the well of relationships.

They draw one relationship right after the next, refilling their cup, hoping the next drink will quench their soul's thirst for companionship.

Sadly, each drink misses the spot, never leaving a feeling of satisfaction. Female reader, please understand what Christ is pointing out. Following this method is a form of insanity, which is defined as doing the same thing over and over, expecting a different result.

Christ informs this woman that He can give her water that will not only allow her to never thirst again, but also cause living water to overflow in her life. In all confidence, Christ basically told her that He was the man of her dreams.

This is how men need to respond to this objection. Humbly present yourself through speech and action as not only the one who is able to put your interest's thirsting to an end.

There is a catch! When Christ said this, the Samaritan woman sarcastically replied "Sir, give me this water that I thirst not, neither come hither to draw." (Jhn 4:15) Basically, she said, "Talk is cheap, prove it, give me this water to drink then."

The Samaritan woman did not know who she was talking to, but she was about to have an EXPERIENCE with Christ that would change her life. Her experience with Christ showed her what was wrong with her life, but also revealed Him as the Messiah, the one who can restore her.

Men, the woman whose affections you are trying to win may not know you are sent by God at first glance. Do not get frustrated if she cautiously tests to see if you were sent by God, or the enemy of our soul. To overcome this obstacle, you must follow the footsteps of Christ and allow your interest to have an EXPERIENCE with you. If you do not understand what we mean, let us break it down for you.

Up until the 1950's, women were wooed into marriage much differently than today. If a fella met a nice gal he expressed his interest. Next he did something grand to sweep her off her feet. This revealed to her that he was a man above all men.

Only someone who truly loves and cares for another will go out of their way to prove their feelings are true. Even the biblical figures who served as types of Christ did the same. Samson killed a lion to get to his wife. Jacob spent seven years working for Laban to marry Rachel, but was tricked into marrying Leah. He then worked seven more years to gain the woman that he truly loved. Boaz begged the person who had the rights to marry Ruth to let him marry her instead.

{Andrae Speaking} I myself used this method to gain the affections of Lysbeth who gave me the woman at the well treatment when I expressed my feelings towards her. She hit me with the same line the Samaritain woman gave to Christ. "There are so many guys who want to be with me, what makes you different than any of them?"

A few days after she said that to me, I had the opportunity to prove I was the man God was using to quench her thirst for companionship. I allowed her to have an EXPERIENCE with me that would woo her off her feet.

Lysbeth was to take part in a wedding of one of her family members in Orlando, Florida. She had her hair and nails done, and her gown was prepared. The only thing she needed was a ride to the airport to catch her flight. She called me and asked me to help.

I told her I would take her, always jumping at an opportunity to be with her, but I warned her she needed to get to the airport an hour and a half before her flight. She brushed off my warning saying, "It's only a domestic flight, I can get there 45 minutes before and be ok." I still came to her house early, so I could bring her to the airport at the proper time. She refused to leave early. Eventually, we got to the airport 45 minutes before her scheduled flight.

When she got to the desk the airline rep told her boarding had closed, that she should have checked in an hour earlier. This was bad enough, but there was no option for standby either. She could not even get a refund.

Lysbeth was devastated. All the money she spent on hair, nails, clothes, makeup, and her ticket, were for nothing. On top of that, she feared ruining the wedding she was supposed to walk in. Seeing how devastated she was started to kill me inside.

I decided to be Lysbeth's drink of water, quenching her thirst and causing a fountain to overflow within her. Without thinking I blurted out, "Don't worry about it, I will drive you to Florida right now so that you can make it to the wedding on time."

As soon as the words were spoken it was as if she was resurrected from the dead. She could not believe I would do something as crazy as drive, non-stop from New York to Florida, just for her, especially since she did not know how to drive.

Even more surprising to her was that I was willing to do this with a suspended license. She thought for a bit and refused, seeing that I could get into serious trouble if caught. I wouldn't take no for an answer.

I packed her things back into the car and we started on our 1,100-mile journey; worshiping, singing praises, and studying the Word the entire trip. We got there just in time for her to get prepped and join the wedding party.

I booked a hotel for a few hours, got some sleep, and waited for Lys' call to have me come pick her up. When she called to let me know she was ready, I picked her up from the reception and we headed straight back home, worshiping, singing praises, and studying the Word on the return trip as well.

This was the EXPERIENCE that Lysbeth had with me, which revealed Christ to her, and changed her life forever. This is how she knew, without any doubt, that I was heaven sent. After this experience, she could not resist my advances any longer.

After the Samaritan woman's experience with Christ, she dropped everything she had and ran back to the village. She shouted to all who could hear, "Come, see a man." (Jhn 4:29) She proclaimed to all the men she had been with, and anyone else who would listen, that she was in a relationship with a real man now.

This is the same thing that will happen to all men if they follow Christ's method for gaining the affections of the woman He draws to them. When another man tries to seduce her she will say, "Come, see a real man." When her friends are discussing their issues with the men they are dating, she will tell them, "Come, see a real man."

To be this man you must walk as Christ walked, and talk and Christ talked. (1 Jhn 2:6) To have this experience you must desire to be like Jesus Christ. This is the true measure of a man.

Ladies, if we wait patiently on the Lord while guarding your affections, and testing the spirits, you can experience this as well. Allow the Holy Spirit to lead you to where you can drink living water that will over flow in your life.

Those blessed men and women who make it past this point will move into the relationship stage called courtship. If you thought how Christ was reveled in this chapter is exciting, hold on to your seat, this is just the beginning.

5 | *Object Lesson #3 In The Courtyard*

In Exodus chapter 25:8, God commands Moses to build a portable temple so that He may dwell among His people. The children of Israel had recently been delivered from Egypt where they spent 400 years in captivity. During that time they had forgotten about God.

God wanted to have a relationship with His people once again, so He gained their affections by allowing them to have an EXPERIENCE with Him, just as we studied. The amazing experience which captured their affections was the Passover and the parting of the Red Sea.

After this experience, the Children of Israel could say to the Egyptians and idolatrous nations in the hills surrounding the desert, "COME SEE A GOD!" They decided once again to enter a relationship with the God of their forefathers.

Now that God had won their affections, He wanted to take the newly formed relationship to the next level. The relationship stage God and the Children of Israel stepped into here is called courtship.

After a man gains the affections of a woman they start a time of learning together. They enter a relationship that focuses on learn about each other while building towards marriage. The two individuals have committed to working together to get to this result.

Even though we do not see "courtship" anywhere in the bible, it is the biblical way to build a relationship. It is this method which Jesus Christ uses to build His relationship with all believers.

God instructed Moses to build His temple so He could dwell among His people. God the Father wanted to draw the bride of Christ to Him through the sanctuary. God the Father did this by using every piece of material incorporated in the building of the sanctuary, and the furniture that was placed inside of it, as a symbol of Christ and the Gospel. From the measurements, to the screws, to the very foundations, everything in that temple represented Christ.

It is in the sanctuary we get to know all that there is to know about Christ, which is why the Psalmist says "Thy way, O God, is in the sanctuary." (Psm 77:13) Everything we need to know about God can be found studying the old testament sanctuary. Every book of the bible is built on the foundation of this structure. Also, as everything in the sanctuary represents Him, Jesus used it to reveal himself to those He ministered to. Let us take a quick walk through the sanctuary to see for ourselves.

There were three compartments in the sanctuary: the Courtyard, Holy Place, and Most Holy Place. The presence of God resided in the Most Holy Place, in the midst of the Israelite camp.

There was only one entrance, or door, to the sanctuary. This is where the Israelites would pass through to engage in the services that brought about salvation and communion with God the Father.

Jesus Christ said, "I am the door; by me if any man enter in, he shall be saved." (Jhn 10:9) This single entrance represented that there is only one way to salvation. "Jesus saith unto him, I am the way, the truth, and the life: no man cometh unto the Father, but by me." John 14:6

Walking through the door, we find ourselves in the courtyard which has two pieces of furniture in it. The first is the alter of burnt offering. Here lambs were sacrificed for the sins of the people. Knowing Jesus Christ is the "Lamb of God, which taketh away the sin of the world," (Jhn 1:29) it is clear the lamb represents Jesus and the altar represents the Cross.

After the altar is a piece of furniture called the laver, which is a large bronze basin filled with water. Think back to the previous chapter where Christ was offering living water to the woman at the well. Can you picture it now?

Now we move into the second compartment, called the Holy Place. There we see three pieces of furniture. The table of Shewbread is first. The priest would place two stacks of unleavened bread on this table.

Unleavened bread is a type of bread that has no yeast in it. Leaven, or yeast, was often used as a symbol for sin. Just as a little yeast spreads through bread, causing it to rise when cooked, a little sin spreads through the soul in the same manner.

Christ, who lived without sin (no leaven), called himself "The bread of life." (Jhn 6:35) Christ is the word made flesh, we symbolically eat the bread of life by studying the Bible.

Next we notice the seven-branched candle stand. This candle stand is used to represent Jesus as "the light of the world." (Jhn 8:12) This lamp also represents the Word of God, "Thy word is a lamp unto my feet, and a light unto my path." (Psalm 119:105)

The last piece of furniture in the Holy Place is the altar of incense. The smoke and aroma from the incense represents the righteous sacrifice of Jesus Christ. Paul tells us, "And walk in love, as Christ also hath loved us, and hath given himself for us an offering and a sacrifice to God for a sweetsmelling savour." (Ephesians 5:2)

Finally, we part the veil and enter the Most Holy Place, also known as the throne room. Here we find the propitiation (covering), or mercy seat. This represents Christ in a beautiful way, "He is the propitiation for our sins, and not for ours only, but also for the sins of the whole world." (1 Jhn 2:2)

We now see how each piece of furniture represents Christ and our relationship to him, let us double back into the courtyard. In the courtyard we begin our courtship experience with Christ. Through the gospel messages found in this compartment, we find instructions for earthly courtships as well.

When an individual has their first EXPERIENCE with God, they really do not know much about Him. The experience builds a desire to know more about this Christ that loves them so much.

Here, the new believer can take some time to get to know the Lord. Not His laws and statutes, but rather who God is, His character. The new believer gets to know God in preparation for the second coming (marriage of the lamb).

This is the same way a man and woman must enter into courtship. Both have the understanding they are getting to know each other better. They share a mindset of marriage as the purpose of this process.

The two pieces of furniture (alter of burnt offering, laver) found in the courtyard give both Christ and the new believer a better understanding of each other. They can also help individuals in a courtship do the same with each other.

As stated earlier, the Altar of Burnt Offering represents the Cross of Christ. Looking at the cross, we see the unconditional love of Jesus Christ. Christ tells us Himself, there is no love like His saying, "Greater love hath no man than this, that a man lay down his life for his friends." (John 15:13)

God loved us so much He laid down His life for us. Our question to the men courting or thinking about courting is, would you be able to lay down your life for this woman? This is something you must ask yourselves while in this relationship stage.

We know you may be ready to close the book right about now, saying to yourself, "This isn't biblical." Well, we will let Paul reinforce the statement for us "Husbands, love your wives, even as Christ also loved the church, and gave himself for it." (Ephesians 5:25) Men, you are called to lay down your life for your wife. This is not something you learn while married. This is a decision that is made while courting the women you are to marry.

For the women reading this, we can imagine you are hollering "PREACH, PREACH!!!!" out loud or in your mind right now, but there are instructions for you as well. Direct your mind to Christ's expected response from a new believer, who realizes that He died for their sins.

God is expecting respect and submission from this new believer. Nothing less could be expected for someone who shed their blood for another. This is the same kind of respect and submission that you must be willing to give to the man that you are to marry.

"Wives, submit yourselves unto your own husbands, as unto the Lord. For the husband is the head of the wife, even as Christ is the head of the church: and he is the savior of the body." (Ephesians 5:22-23) God expects a woman who is joined to a man after God's own heart to walk side-by-side with him, wherever he leads. This is the submission Paul is speaking of here. Remember, the definition of a help meet is a woman who helps her husband fulfill his God given purpose.

The question women must ask themselves while courting is, "Is God leading this man?" If you can see the hand of God in his life, you can rest easy knowing that you will find joy in submission.

This is why many marriages fail. There are a lot of women who do not want to submit. In failing to submit women take away the purpose of a man, the very thing God created him for. If he loses his purpose with you, he will be unhappy in the relationship. This usually ends with the man finding someone who will happily give him the respect he is looking for. This new friendship majority of the time, leads to him cheating, or even divorcing his wife altogether. But happy is the man whose wife allows him to function in the role God created him to have. There is no reason for him to seek love from another, or to leave at all, if he can function as he was created (unless he is not submitted to God).

We know there is a great fear in women when the respect or submission words come around. Most woman begin to fear they will be treated as slaves, and the man will walk all over them.

This is where the man LOVES THE WOMAN INTO SUBMISSION. Look at it while considering the new believer and Christ. The new believer desires to leave a life of sin because they have experienced the unconditional love of God. Christ does not treat the new believer as a slave, but loves them. This leads the new believer to submit willfully to Christ.

How many of us have heard Satan whispering in our ears, "your sin is too great, you should be ashamed of yourself!!!!!!! God will never take you back!!!!!" The word of God comforts us, telling us this is a lie. "But God commendeth his love toward us, in that, while we were yet sinners, Christ died for us." (Romans 5:8) This shows us, even though we did the thing which we are too ashamed to tell anyone else about, Christ saw our sins from Calvary and died for us anyway.

The joy of forgiveness and the feeling of unconditional love, when we know we deserve much worse, takes our hearts captive, driving us to say, "Lord, whatever you want me to say, I will say. Whatever you want me to do, I will do. Wherever you want me to go, I will go." This is how a man is to love his wife into submission.

Ladies, a man that shows he loves you as much as he loves himself is the kind of man you should never be ashamed, or afraid, to submit to. "So ought men to love their wives as their own bodies. He that loveth his wife loveth himself. For no man ever yet hated his own flesh; but nourisheth and cherisheth it, even as the Lord the church." (Ephesians 5:28-29)

When courting a man that shows this characteristic, submission should be a joy to to give. Understand too, women who refuse to humble themselves will be humbled eventually, while those who obey will be exalted. Queen Esther humbled herself before King Ahasuerus and this is how he responded, "What wilt thou, queen

Esther? And what is thy request? It shall be even given thee to the half of the kingdom." (Esther 5:3)

Looking at the other side of the spectrum, we see the woman who held the crown before Esther, Queen Vashti. She serves as an example of all women who are too proud to be submissive. King Ahasuerus sent for her to come to his feast so that he could show his guest the beauty of his wife. Lead by her pride, She refused the kings command, being unwilling to submit to him. In Queen Vashti's prideful act she, while throwing a party for the wives of the princes of Persia, she made an incredible statement to her guests.

She showed them they did not need to submit to their husbands. When the princes that were in the King's feast heard of this, they knew if Queen Vashti was not punished for her actions their wives would begin to disrespect them as well. They said amongst themselves, "For this deed of the queen shall come abroad unto all women, so that they shall despise their husbands in their eyes, when it shall be reported, the King Ahasuerus commanded Vashti the queen to be brought in before him, but she came not. Likewise shall the ladies of Persia and Media say this day unto all the king's princes, which have heard of the deed of the queen. Thus shall there arise too much contempt and wrath." (Esther 1:17-18)

The Princes of Persia had a valid point regarding the effect Queens Vashti's example would have on women in the land. In modern times, young daughters grow to believe submission is a strange thing, because they never saw it in their mother.

Single and married women are continuously fed this mindset by society as the feminist movement is promoted throughout every form of main stream media, EVEN CARTOONS. Worst of all, this movement has crept its way into the Christian church!

The examples of women against the biblical teaching of submission have had a major influence on the women of today. Submission is something that is not seen as the norm, but rather an outdated practice, coming from an ancient time where women had no rights and kept silent.

This allows Satan to have such a strangle hold on marriage and the home. Though it is not the main reason for the insanely high divorce rate, it is a contributing factor. If only we would apply the gospel's remedy to these issues in our lives, we would see it immediately simplify them.

This is the same Gospel that shows a man and woman what true submission is through Jesus Christ. Christ Himself submits to his Heavenly Father, yet He can still claim equality with His father.

Why was it so easy for Jesus to submit? The gospel shows us the unconditional love of God the Father drove Christ to submission. "The father loveth the Son, and hath given all things into his hands." (John 3:35)

Here we see a resemblance in the action of King Ahasuerus, giving all things into the hands of Esther, with God the Father doing the same for His Son. In the same way a man should give all the love he has into the hands of his wife.

The examples of Esther and Vashti show how God will exalt women who obey Him and submit to their husbands, while humbling those who are too prideful to do so. This is also an example of how a man should love his wife into submission, treating her in the same manner he would treat himself.

Yes, we know this is a little much to grasp all at once, but this is what we must look for and think about while in a courtship. You may also be saying to yourself, "This is too hard for me to do."

For the man that has an issue with giving unconditional love, and the woman who has a problem with submission, the next stage in courtship with the new believer and Christ show where you get the power to do this.

As their knowledge of the character of Christ grows, the new believer understands there are changes to make in their life if they desire a committed relationship with Jesus to develop. In their heart, the new believer wants to make these changes. Unfortunately they struggle, having lived a certain way so long that caused them to grow accustomed to yielding to their flesh. Naturally, a war between yielding to Christ and yielding to the flesh ensues. Of this fight Paul says, "For the flesh lusteth against the Spirit, and the Spirit against the flesh: and these are contrary the one to the other: so that ye cannot do the things that ye would." (Galatians 5:17)

In the courtship experience with Jesus Christ, new believers come to a struggle between the flesh and the Spirit. Paul himself experienced this struggle stating, "For the good that I would I do not: but the evil which I would not, that I do." (Romans 7:19)

Thankfully, God gives Paul the answer and renews hope amidst the struggle in one powerful sentence. "My grace is sufficient for thee: for my strength is made perfect in weakness." (2 Corinthians 12:9)

Romans 1:5 tells us the grace of God instills within us the ability to obey and have faith in him. There is a catch though. Paul tell us we must die to our flesh to experience this. How often must we die to our flesh? In telling us to follow his example Paul says, "I die daily." (1 Corinthians 15:31)

The next question may be, "What do you mean by, dying to your flesh?" Well, this means that we understand our weakness; that we are unable to change ourselves and attain righteousness on our own. At this point, we recognize our need for Jesus to save us.

It is at this point we learn that our salvation is found in coming to the cross. This is why Paul teaches by example, "I am crucified with Christ nevertheless I live; yet not I but Christ liveth in me: and the life which I now live in the flesh I live by the faith of the Son of God, who loved me, and gave himself for me." (Galatians 2:20)

Reader, this is the same experience that you are to have in a courtship. Men, you will overcome your inability to love unconditionally when you make it your mission to be crucified with Christ daily, so that this love can be given by the power of Jesus Christ who lives in you.

Women, you can freely give the respect of submission when you make it your duty to daily die to yourselves, allowing Christ to take his rightful place on the throne of your heart.

With Christ living in you, you gain the ability to do good. Good which you will find insanely hard to do by your own strength. In this situation, the good is unconditional love for the man and submission for the woman.

This is what we are to look for and aspire to in a courtship, especially one following the model the gospel provides. If Christ and these qualities are visibly present in our lives, and the lives of the individuals we are interested in, we may be close to taking the next step in our relationship journey.

So it is with the new believer, who is now set to move to the next stage of courtship with Christ, which is associated with the laver. The laver represents the word of God as the living water that cleanses and fills us.

"Wherewithal shall a young man cleanse his way? By taking heed thereto according to thy word. With my whole heart have I sought thee: O let me not wander from thy commandments." (Psalm 119:9-10)

Those in courtships should seek God together through diligent study of his Word and constant prayer, just as a new believer must. They should constantly ask Him what His Will is for the both of them. They should seek out Spirit-led counselors to help with this decision as well. The more you seek God out on the matter, desiring to do His will only, the clearer He will make sure to answer you.

Also, both parties need to accept whatever answer God gives, whether it brings joy or pain. Our faith in His ability to guide us to happiness is what truly makes God happy.

Hold dear these words of Paul, "But without faith it is impossible to please Him: for he that commeth to God must believe that he is, and that he is a rewarder of them that diligently seek him." (Hebrews 11:6)

This is the essence of righteousness by faith, which is the only way to salvation. Having faith in God's gender roles will lead to a righteous marriage. Having faith that God will guide our decision on whether or not to be engaged, leads to marriages where divorce is not even a thought, much less an option.

If you are struggling with taking this as truth, please, prayerfully study the gospel in connection to marriage. You will find that we are not speaking of ourselves, but only giving our testimony of the Gospel of Jesus Christ.

But, if you have seen Jesus clearly in what you have just read, continue on to the next stage of the relationship journey. After a successful courtship is the excitement of the engagement period. Understanding how the love of God is seen in this stage will blow your mind.

6 | Object Lesson #4
No Greater Proposal Than This

Have you ever wondered where our marriage customs came from? Seriously, have you ever sat back and pondered who came up with proposals, or wedding ceremonies? Being that marriage is an institution set up by God, does scripture have anything to say about this?

In this day and age we have become mindless sheep, following trends promoted by the media, no questions asked. Whatever Facebook or Twitter says is fashionable and trending, the whole world follows without a thought.

Marriage is something that plays a major factor in your soul salvation. (Remember Samson, and being unequally yoked?) It is important to question everything. Let us search scripture to find the answer to the question, why do we do all of this?

MODERN DAY PROPOSAL

The standing tradition for a proposal is a man professing his undying love for the woman he is in a relationship with. This profession of love is his public declaration of the commitment he is willing to make and is usually done in the presence of family, friends, and maybe even strangers.

The man leaves himself vulnerable and open to shame if the woman rejects his proposal in front of everyone. Sadly, many men have experienced this crushing blow, some even on live television (Ouch).

The woman publicly declares her love by accepting the proposal in front of everyone. This is a proclamation to the world that the two have made a commitment, or engagement rather, for marriage.

The man then provides the woman with an engagement ring. This is a sign the woman is taken, set to be married. This sums up the well-known tradition practiced around the world today.

BIBLICAL HEBREW PROPOSAL

In biblical times, the Israelites practiced something similar, but with a few twists. When a man proposed to a woman, he would offer her a cup of wine (grape juice) to drink. If the woman drank the juice, it meant she accepted the proposal.

This was done publicly, amongst family and friends, as a declaration to all of the commitment being made. As you can see, the difference between the custom then and now is no bending on one knee and giving an engagement ring.

After this, the male's family would give a dowry, or pay a price, to the woman's family (owner). The father, or the heads of the family, determined the amount of the dowry. There were various reasons this was done.

Daughters played a vital role in the house of their fathers, whether it was maintaining the house, or a business purposes. With the daughter now gone, it often proved a decisive blow to the order of the father's house. For this reason, the woman's father would set a price he thought would cover the loss he incurred giving his daughter away. Looking closely, we can see this throughout the bible.

When Abraham's servant found Rebekah he paid a dowry to the head of the family, her brother Laban. "And the servant brought forth jewels of sliver and jewels of gold, and raiment, and gave them to Rebekah: he gave also to her brother and to her mother precious things." (Genesis 24:53)

Isaac's son Jacob did not have his father around to pay his dowry for him. Instead he had to work it off. After running away from home, he came to Laban's house for refuge. There he sees Rachel, the daughter of his uncle, asking him for her hand in marriage. To pay the dowry Jacob agreed to work seven years for Laban, after which the marriage could ensue.

We know how the story goes, Laban tricked Jacob into working for and marrying Leah. This caused Jacob to work another seven years to pay a dowry for Rachel so he could marry the woman that he loved.

We have presented to you two cases in which a dowry was paid. In the first, Abraham provided the payment for the dowry, a gift for his son. Then there is Jacob, who tried working off the dowry himself, which did not end too well for him.

You might find it interesting to see this custom pointed the eyes of all who followed it to the plan of salvation. It is by this very system that salvation is afforded to all who sincerely desire it.

REVEALING CHRIST

We believe if you, the reader, think very hard, you will begin to see how this custom maps out the plan of salvation. Just think really hard for a moment. Is there a practice that happens every so often at your church where you drink a cup of grape juice?

Has the light gone off in your head yet? Yes, the communion service points back to Jesus Christ proposing to us. This is the practice we receive from the last supper, where Christ spoke of this cup of grape juice saying "This cup is the new testament in my blood, which is shed for you." (Luke 22:20)

Do you also understand why Christ's first miracle was performed at a wedding, in turning water into wine? This was a foreshadowing of what He came to do, proposing to the woman He came to woo, the church.

Christ's first miracle also shows that His proposal is far greater than any proposal there ever was, or ever will be. The words spoken by the governor of the wedding feast, regarding the wine Jesus created show us how great it was. In speaking to the bridegroom, the governor said, "Every man at the beginning doth set forth good wine; and when men have well drunk, then that which is worse: but thou has kept the good wine until now." (John 2:10)

The governor did not know it was Jesus who performed this miracle, only the servants who helped Christ knew the truth. The wine Jesus provides to us is far greater than any we can receive elsewhere.

Christ's cup of wine is far better a proposal than any other for this simple reason. Christ, in a public display of love, put Himself to "open shame" (Heb 6:6), hanging naked from a cross. It was there, in a public declaration of love, He imparted His blood to us, proposing to us.

There is no greater proposal than this, because there is no greater a love than this. It was not enough for Christ to get on bended knee, rather, He laid Himself out before us. More than that, He did this despite the possible humiliation of rejection.

But wait, isn't there a dowry to pay? Yes, there is! Did you know that because of sin, Satan has rightful claim to our souls, as if we are his children? Sounds crazy right? But Christ proves this to be true as He proclaimed to the wicked Pharisee's "Ye are of your father the devil." (John 8:44)

Just as a daughter worked as a type of servant in her father's (master of the household) home, all who live in sin are servants to the master of sin. "Know ye not that to whom ye yield yourselves servants to obey, his servants ye are to whom ye obey; wheher of sin unto death, or obedience unto righteousness." (Romans 6:16)

We all have sinned. We have all lived as children and servants of our soul's enemy at some point in time, and a dowry is needed to free us from this house of sin. God the Father paid this dowry on our behalf through His Son, Jesus Christ.

"For God so loved the world that he gave his only begotten Son, that whosoever believeth in him should not perish but have everlasting life." (John 3:16) God the Father gave His greatest treasure of all as a dowry for us.

Again, this dowry was first represented by Abraham giving gifts to Laban and to Rebekah's mother on Isaac's behalf. In the same manner, we must understand the dowry paid on our behalf is a Gift from God which is "eternal life through Jesus Christ." (Romans 6:23)

This helps us understand why Jacob had such a problem trying to pay his own dowry. In the sin of deceiving his father and gaining his birthright by his own works, just like Abraham having a son with his handmaid, Jacob began to live by his own righteousness. Jacob did not trust God would give him the birthright he was divinely promised, so he went out to get it himself. With this same mindset, he tried to pay Rachel's dowry by his own works.

The lesson we learn here is that we cannot save ourselves from, or pay the ransom price for, our sins. "All Our righteousness are as filthy rags." (Is 64:6) By this we learn, we need the righteousness of Jesus Christ which alone can pay our sin debt.

As Jesus Christ proposed to us in a public declaration of love. How do we accept this proposal? The answer is plain and simple, BAPTISM. Baptism is generally done before your church congregation, family, and friends as you devote your life to Jesus Christ.

In this process we go into the watery grave, being crucified with Christ. We receive our engagement ring in the form of the cross they are symbolically supposed to bear. All who are engaged to Christ are expected to take up their cross. (Mat 16:24)

As we bear this cross to the world, by showing the character of Christ in our daily lives, we become known as individuals who are in a relationship with Him. This is the same way a woman engaged to be married can be identified, by looking at her engagement ring.

YOUR COMMITMENT

Do you see proposals in a new light? Do you recognize the commitment you are making? By the man proposing, he is declaring to give his life over to another. By accepting, the woman is declaring the same.

When we become engaged to be married, our demeanor and character must change. We are no longer the single guy or girl that lives life for themselves. It is almost as if we are born again, a new person.

Our walk and talk changes. We do not entertain certain conversations or actions with the opposite sex. By displaying this new character, and a sign that we may bear, all know that we are engaged to be married.

What an awesome custom God created, allowing the gospel to be imprinted in our minds. It is our hope that if you have never seen the gospel this way before you let it burn in your mind today, especially when it comes time for you to experience this for yourself.

7 | *Object Lesson #5*
Prepping For A New Life

The season of engagement is a wonderful but busy time. The two individuals that are committed to be married, experience the joyous blessing of finding the one God has prepared for them.

Yet, it is a stressful time because there is so much to prepare for and so little time to do it. Many times, during engagement, the two may be so excited they forget to prepare for life after the wedding. Even worse, they may not know how to prepare for it at all.

Fortunately, as has been shown throughout this book, the gospel is a wonderful simplifier of all our issues and confusions. If we really want to know what to do in preparation for the wedding, we look no further than Jesus Christ.

We are told throughout scripture that we are waiting on the "Marriage of the Lamb." If this is so, it means that we, along with Christ, are in the engagement phase as we speak. This means we can look to the gospel for instructions on how we must prepare for this event with Christ.

PREPERATION FOR THE MAN

Every man that has gone through the engagement and wedding prep phase knows they have very little say in planning for the day. Even so, their presence is still expected during the planning (seeing venues, food tastings, etc.).

They know their input is not needed, but their interest in the process makes their future wife happy. Most men just want a dapper suit and their best mates behind them on their wedding day.

The man's real focus is the day after the wedding, the day when real life begins. Men are not generally as caught up in the magic of the moment. They are entering a time in life where they are now responsible to provide for another human being. There is so much responsibility on the table, and such a short time to prepare for it. One of the biggest of all the reasonability's is providing a place to bring the woman back to after the wedding.

Depending on the time between the engagement and wedding, the man must figure out how and where he will provide shelter for himself and his wife. His focus becomes, more so than everything else, preparing a place for his bride.

In biblical times, when a Hebrew man's proposal was accepted, this was also his main focus. The man would leave his fiancé for a time. He would head to his father's house (land), where he would build a house for himself and his bride.

Before he left he would console his bride, who would surely miss him. He made sure there was no reason for the bride to worry because she knew where he was. She understood the custom, and if there was any emergency in which she needed him, she knew the way to him.

If you have not drawn the parallel to the gospel, let us draw it out for you. Christ proposed to us on the cross, and we accepted His proposal through baptism. After His crucifixion, Christ rose again, and returned to the home of His Father in heaven.

Before Christ left, He gave His bride-to-be this wonderful assurance, "Let not your heart be troubled: ye believe in God, believe also in me. In my father's house are many mansions: if it were not so, I would have told you. I go to prepare a place for you. And if I go and prepare a place for you, I will come again, and receive you unto myself; that where I am, there ye may be also. And whither I go ye know, and the way ye know." (John 14:1-4)

Christ's focus is not really on the wedding, but on the life to come after the wedding. For this reason, He has gone to prepare quarters for His bride. As he has left to do this, He gives us assurance, telling us not to worry. He does not want us saddened by His absence, leaving a sure promise that He will come again, and take us back to where He is.

Through the gospel, we see that the man's man focus is the future provision for his bride. This is not just associated with a home, but the preparation and execution of a well thought out plan for life after the wedding.

During the engagement, many couples get a sickness called "Wedding Fever" which keeps them from looking past the day of the marriage. For most women, this is almost impossible to avoid, as their wedding is something they have been dreaming of since they were seven years old. This is why the man is given this responsibility as his emotions are not completely engrossed with the event. Fortunately, we can still pull a spiritual application from the mindset of the woman.

PREPERATION FOR THE WOMAN

As we discussed, most woman get so engrossed in the wedding preparation and day, they lose sight of the life that is to come afterwards. One of the major points of focus for the bride, is choosing the perfect wedding dress for the day. Take heart, this is not a bad thing. This is how God designed it. The wedding gown being the greatest focus of the bride serves as a sermon.

As much as a bride focuses on a wedding dress today, in biblical times the wedding gown was the Hebrew woman's point of focus just the same. The wedding itself was set up by the parents, leaving the bride to focus on her dress and making sure she was prepared for the wedding.

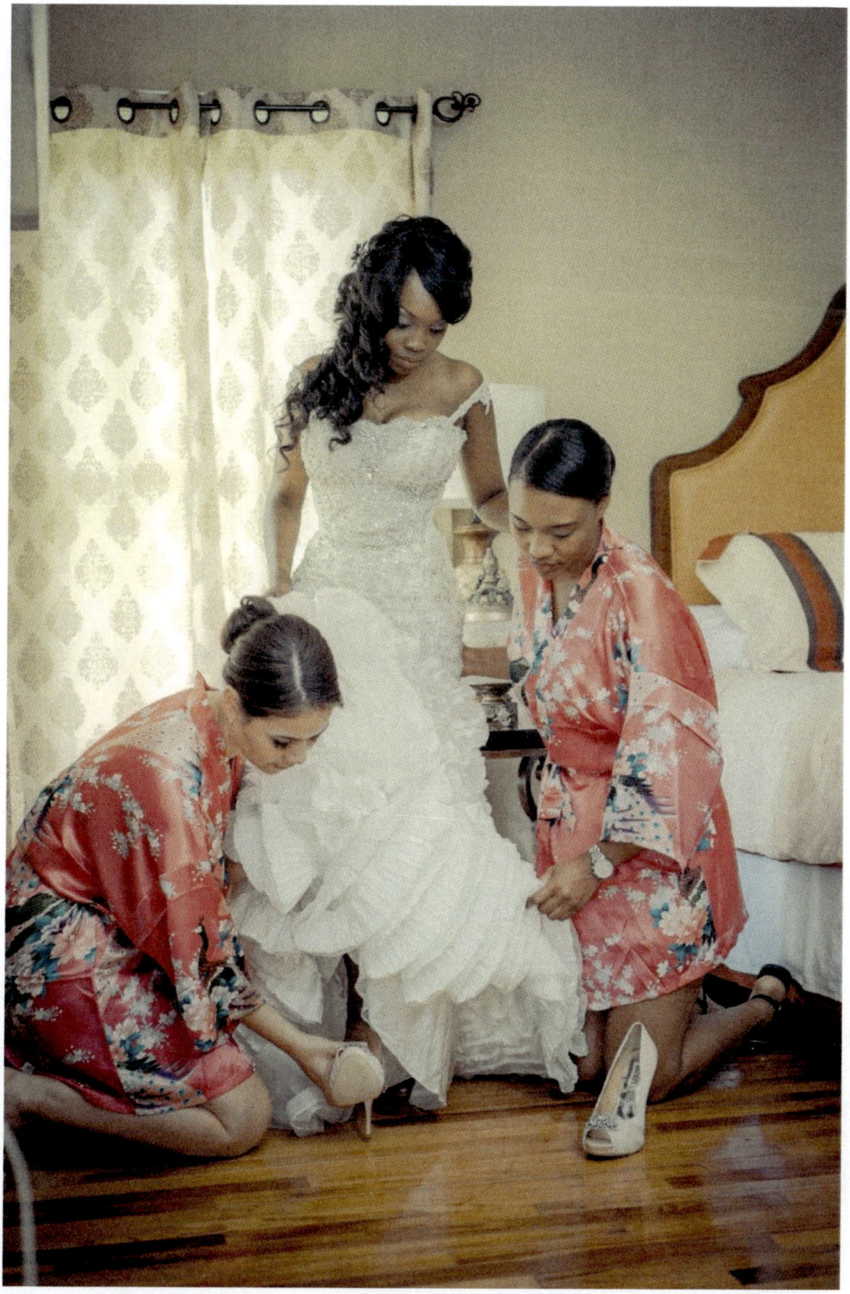

The bride's focus served a purpose. When her future husband finished preparing their house, he would make a call that the wedding was supposed to start. This may sound crazy to a lot of women, but yes, there was not date set for the wedding. The wedding could start at any time. This uncertainty is why the bride only focused on her responsibility for the wedding day. The bridegroom took care of the future.

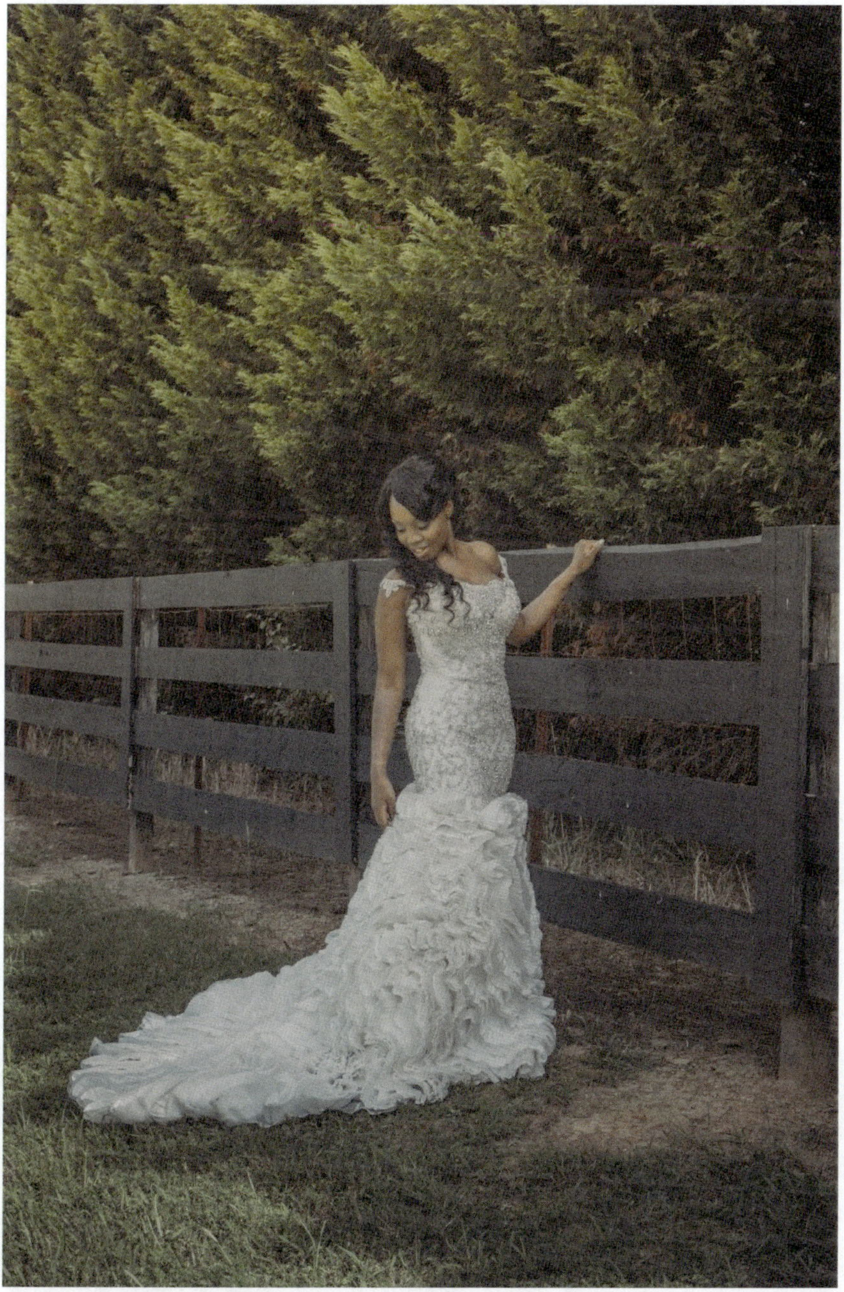

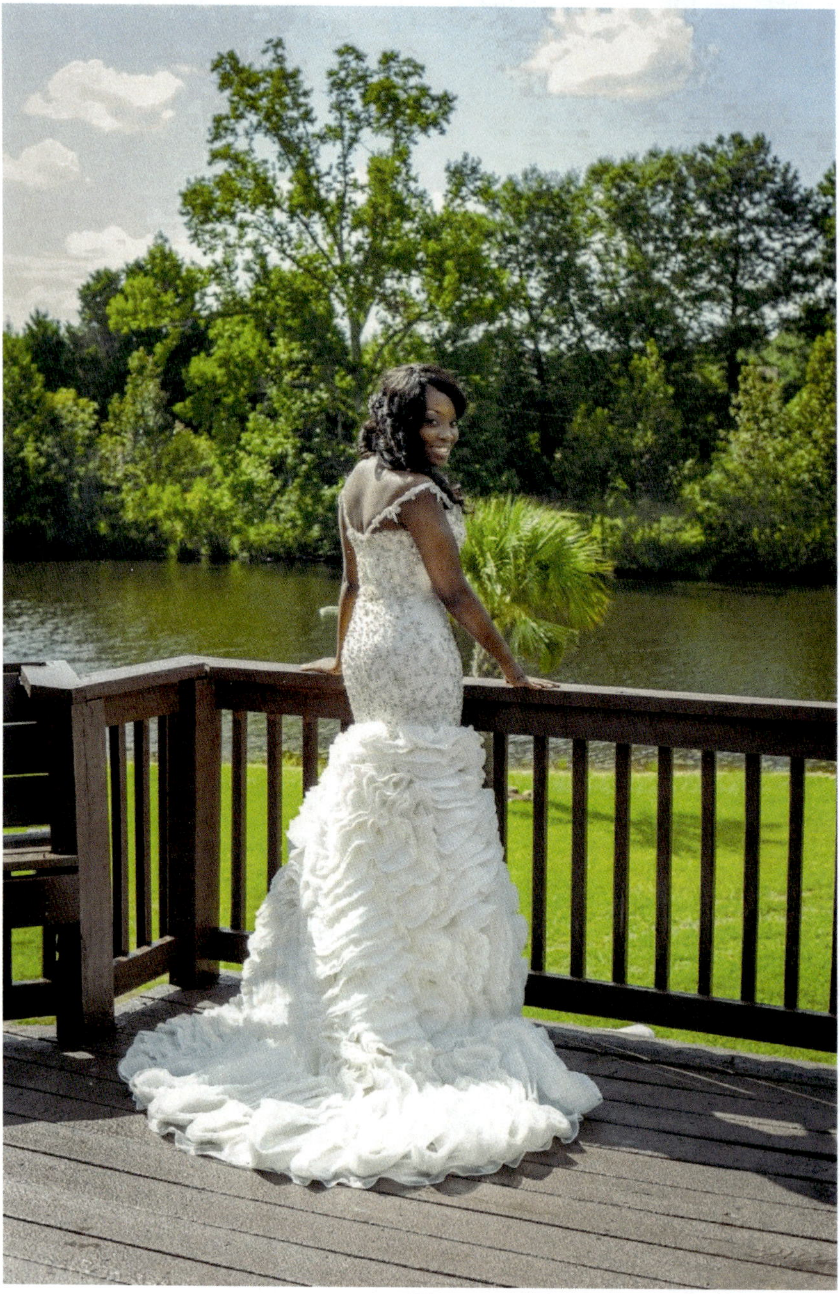

Since the bridegroom could call at any time, the woman had to be ready every day. She prepared as if the bridegroom was to show up at any moment. This brings to mind the parable of the ten virgins.

The ten virgins are a symbol of the church as one body. Ten is a symbolic number in the bible that represents a remnant, or left overs. This remnant is who Jesus Christ is coming back for. "And the dragon (satan) was wroth with the woman, and went to make war with the remnant of her seed, which keep the commandments of God, and have the testimony of Jesus Christ." (Revelation 12:17)

Here we see that this remnant which came from the woman, or early church (as a woman is a symbol for the church in prophecy), keep the commandments of God and have the testimony of Jesus Christ. We are told that the testimony of Jesus is "the spirit of prophecy." (Rev 19:10)

We get a better picture of this remnant through John's vision of them in Revelation chapter 14. Here are a few identifying marks of the remnant as told to John while he was on the Isle of Patmos.

The remnant were spiritual VIRGINS, which mean they have not served any other gods or false doctrines. (Rev 14:4) They have the name of God the Father and Jesus Christ symbolically written on their foreheads, which means they harbor the Character of God the Father and His Son (engagement ring given to us by Christ; reread chapter 6). (Rev 14:1) Finally, they keep the commandments and have the faith of Jesus Christ. (Rev 14:12) This is the same description that is found of the remnant in Revelation chapter 19. What we are reading of is the people of God who have made themselves ready to meet the Lord, the TRUE CHURCH.

In his effort to prepare the Christian church of his day and ours for our wedding with Christ, The Apostle Paul Says this, "For I am jealous over you with a godly jealousy: for I have espoused you to one husband, that I may present you as a chaste virgin to Christ." (2 Corinthians 11:2)

If those who experience marriage with the Lord are to be spiritual virgins, what signifies to the bridegroom, and wedding guests, that the bride is a virgin? It is a pure WHITE DRESS that signifies this.

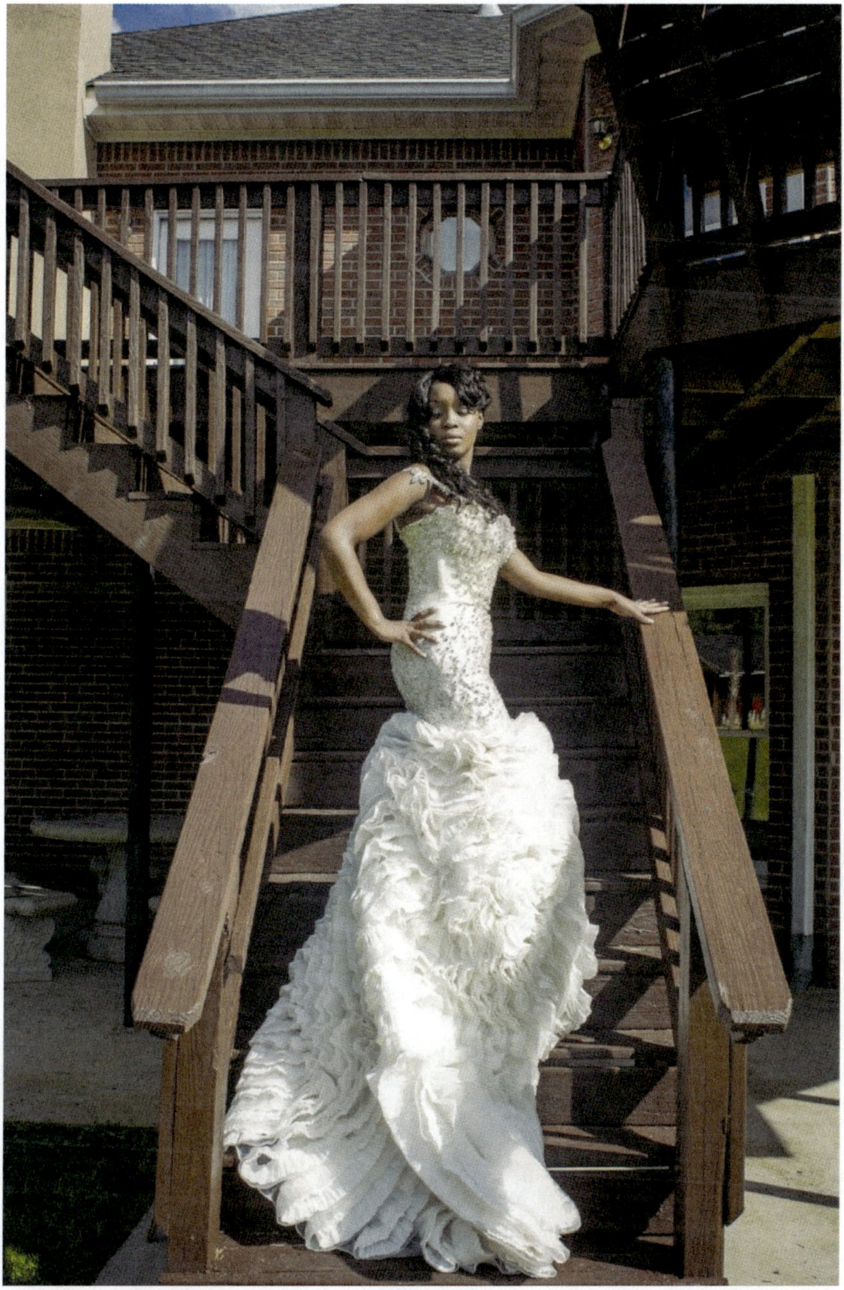

This is what Paul is trying to help the church prepare. Without the white gown, we will not enter the wedding. Christ gave a parable of a wedding guest that did not have on the proper attire at the wedding feast of a King's son.

Christ explains the fate of this unprepared guest by saying, "And when the king came in to see the guests, he saw there a man which had not a wedding garment. And he saith unto him, Friend, how camest thou in hither not having a wedding garment? And he was speechless. Then said the king to the servants, Bind him hand and foot, and take him away, and cast him into outer darkness; there shall be weeping and gnashing of teeth." (Matthew 22:11-13)

This is a picture of all those who will not be prepared for the wedding. They will hear the bridegroom's call, but they will not prepare themselves for the wedding. This is the reason for the bride to make her dress and other preparations her main focus.

Similarly, Christ warns us to keep oil in our lamps. The lamp represents the word of God, as the Psalmist says, "Thy word is a lamp unto my feet, and a light unto my path." (Psalm 119:105) The oil found inside the lamp is the anointing of the Holy Spirit.

Only the Holy Spirit points out and reveals the truth of the Word to us. Also, we cannot hold to, or keep, the commandments of God by our own strength. We can only do it by the power of Christ, in the form of the Holy Spirit in us.

The five foolish virgins are those in the church who know about truth, but they have not surrendered to, or received, the indwelling of the Holy Spirit for one reason or the other. Without the Spirit, it is impossible for them to keep the commandments or embody the faith of Jesus Christ. They did not make themselves ready and will be cast into outer darkness, like the wedding guest who was not prepared for the wedding. As they begged the bridegroom to let them in to the wedding chamber (symbol of heaven) he said, "Verily I say unto you, I know you not." (Matthew 25:12)

The five foolish virgins were kept in the outer darkness they were seeking salvation from, all because they did not prepare. Do you see why it is important for the bride to focus on her wedding preparations?

At the marriage of the lamb this is what was said of the five wise virgins, "Let us be glad and rejoice, and give honour to him: for the marriage of the lamb is come, and his wife hath made herself ready. And to her was granted that she should be arrayed in fine linen, clean and white: for the fine linen is the righteousness of saints. And he saith unto me, Write, Blessed are they which are called unto the marriage supper of the Lamb. And he saith unto me, these are the true sayings of God." (Revelation 19:7-9)

PRACTICAL APPLICATION

Christ is preparing a home for his bride, the church. His example shows the man's responsibility is to focus on preparing a home for his bride here on earth, after the wedding. Also, men, do not be upset by how engrossed in the wedding your fiancé is.

Point her eyes to the spiritual application of it all. Show her how you should both have the same kind of excitement for the marriage of the lamb. Show her how you should both prepare your garments from now.

The real wedding is yet to come!!! The question is, have you received the Holy Spirit? Are you standing on the foundation of God's Word? Do you hold true to the commandments of God, all ten?

When we stand on the foundation of God's Word the Holy Spirit leads and guides us through our bible study. By the Holy Spirit we gain understanding of the prophecies in the bible. With this knowledge, we can better prepare for the second coming of Jesus Christ.

Reader, whether you look towards your wedding, are preparing for one, or have completed yours already, look to this relationship stage as a symbol of how you and your significant other can prepare yourselves spiritually today, so you are ready when Christ, our bridegroom, calls.

8 | *Object Lesson #8*
The Day

We have made it all the way to the wedding day, the journey to marriage is almost complete. All the while Jesus Christ has been at the center of it all. Since we have come this far carried by the faith of Jesus, let Him carry us all the way to the finish line.

Just like proposals, weddings are filled with traditions that we do not know much about, but we follow them none the less. With the knowledge we have gained so far, it would be safe to say we will find elements of the gospel in these traditions.

CLOSE FAMILY AND FRIENDS

A bride and groom both have individuals they want to attend their wedding. These people are their closest friends and family members, who make up the wedding party, and guests.

Looking through the lens of the gospel, we see Christ will bring all of heaven with when He comes for His wedding. "And when he had opened the seventh seal, there was silence in heaven about the space of half an hour." (Revelation 8:1)

John, speaking on the breaking of the last seal of revelation, sees a vision of the second coming of Jesus Christ. In this vision, all of heaven was silent because for the first time, it will be empty. Christ is coming to the wedding with His closest family members and friends.

The bride of Christ (the church) will have spectators as well, but it is much different in this scenario. It is not a good thing to be a part of the bridal party or the other guests, as they will not be leaving with Christ after the wedding.

Our goal is to be the bride, one of the many members of the "True Church" who are all counted as one body in Christ. As we learned throughout this book, the church is symbolized as a virgin woman who is to be espoused to Christ.

REPRESENT YOUR SIDE

Back to our analysis, the first tradition we run into is the separation of allegiances. The wedding party and guests that are in allegiance to the bride sit on one side, while those of the groom are on the other.

When Christ comes back, the Bible shows that His feet will not touch the ground, rather, He will be suspended in the air. There Christ will hold His position at the altar, where He will wait for His beautiful bride to meet Him.

MEETING ON AISLE 1

This is where we see the parallel between the second coming of Jesus Christ, and the tradition of the bride walking down the aisle. When Christ comes to claim His people, both dead and living, His bride will walk down the aisle, ascending to the alter to be by his side. "For the Lord himself shall descend from heaven with a shout, with the voice of the archangel, and with the trump of God: and the dead in Christ shall rise first: then we which are alive and remain shall be caught up together with him in the clouds, to meet the Lord in the air:" (1 Thessalonians 4:16-17)

Men, think about how we will feel, watching our bride walk down the aisle. We have been anticipating this moment since the day we decided she was the one. Just think of all the emotions that will be running through our minds, and the journey that we travelled to reach this moment.

Multiply that by infinity and you will understand the emotions that will run through the mind of Christ. We often see Christ as this supernatural being, void of emotion. This mindset drives us to view the second coming as an event where Christ comes to scoop us up, then bounces back to heaven.

How wrong of a picture can we have of Christ? This is the same loving creator that put the plan of redemption into motion before we were created, knowing that we would sin. Peter tells us He was pre-ordained to die from the foundations of the world. (1 Pet 1:19-20)

Think of His 7,000-year journey to get to this point. Think about the loved ones He lost century after century. Think about the hardships He experienced in His relationship with His people. Think about the suffering, pain, blood, sweat and tears experience from His first advent to the cross.

For Him the journey has finally come to an end. He can once again have face to face communion with His people, His bride. Just imagine what Christ had to go through to get to this point.

Do we not imagine there would be tears in His eyes as He sees His bride walking down this supernatural aisle to Him? This is what should be in the mind of all men, when they see their bride to be, walking towards them.

Women, we paint the same picture in your minds as the men. Imagine how you will feel walking down the aisle. This is something you have dreamed of since you were seven years old.

The moment is finally here. You are to become one with your soul mate. No more failed relationships, giving your feelings to those who do not deserve them. The love of our lives, and a story book beginning, is just a few feet away.

But you need to think beyond this. Think about how you will feel when ascending in the air to meet Christ, face to face. Are we longing to meet Jesus just as much as you are longing for an earthly mate?

Many people say they cannot wait for Jesus to come back, but when they really sit back and think about it, great fear comes upon them. They begin to see the day as a horrific, apocalyptic event.

Will you view Christ when He returns in the same way that you will view your future husband while he is standing at the altar? Will your joy be multiplied in that day more than your actual wedding day?

Reader, if you do not have a similar longing to stand at the altar with Christ, then you need to re-evaluate your relationship with Him. This does not mean that you are a bad person, Christ just wants to take your relationship with Him to a deeper level.

VOWS, LAW, LOVE

The next tradition in line is taking vows. Here the bride and groom swear their love and allegiance to other. They are bound to the laws of marriage. These laws are not seen as grievous because love is the foundation.

This is the same in our relationship with Jesus Christ. If there are laws governing the relationship between a husband and a wife, it makes sense that there are also laws governing our relationship with Christ.

Like a wedding vow, our commitment to Christ should not be based in shrill commandment keeping. Our love for Christ should be so strong, that we desire not to hurt Him. This should be our motivation to keep his laws. This is why Christ says, "If you love me, keep my commandments." (Jhn 14:15)

Not cheating on your spouse does not prove that you love them, rather fidelity is practiced because you love your spouse. Just the same, we should not keep the commandments to prove we love Christ, but rather because we love Christ.

On top of it all, Christ imparts grace to us, which gives us the power to obey and have faith in Him. In turn, Christ's love is so powerful, He places His love in us to love Him back properly, isn't that awesome?

Hopefully, for those who marry, keeping to these laws of love will not be a burden. We mean, if it is a burden, do you really love your spouse? This again parallels our relationship with Christ. If we truly love Him, will obedience to Him be such a burden?

We are told, "For this is the love of God, that we keep his commandments: and his commandments are not grievous." (1Jhn 5:3) The wedding vows are where we see a beautiful picture of JUSTICE & MERCY, LAW & LOVE, coming together in perfect harmony.

The vows taken at the wedding alter are sealed in the Lord, only to be broken by death. It is a commitment to be held for the rest of our existence. This is the same expectation seen at the marriage of the lamb, but with a twist.

Those who are saved will be sealed in their commitment to Him by the name of the Lord. "He that is righteous, let him be righteous still: and he that is holy, let him be holy still." (Revelation 22:11) After this sealing, there is no breaking this commitment. Unlike earthly marriages, the vow cannot be overturned by death. There is no "till death do us part" in heaven, there is only eternity. The vow that we will take is to be forever with the Lord, covered in His righteousness.

THE MAGIC MOMENT

Next is the moment everyone has been waiting for, the kiss. The true tradition associated with this is the two parties avoiding all physical interaction in any way before the wedding. Their first contact would be the kiss.

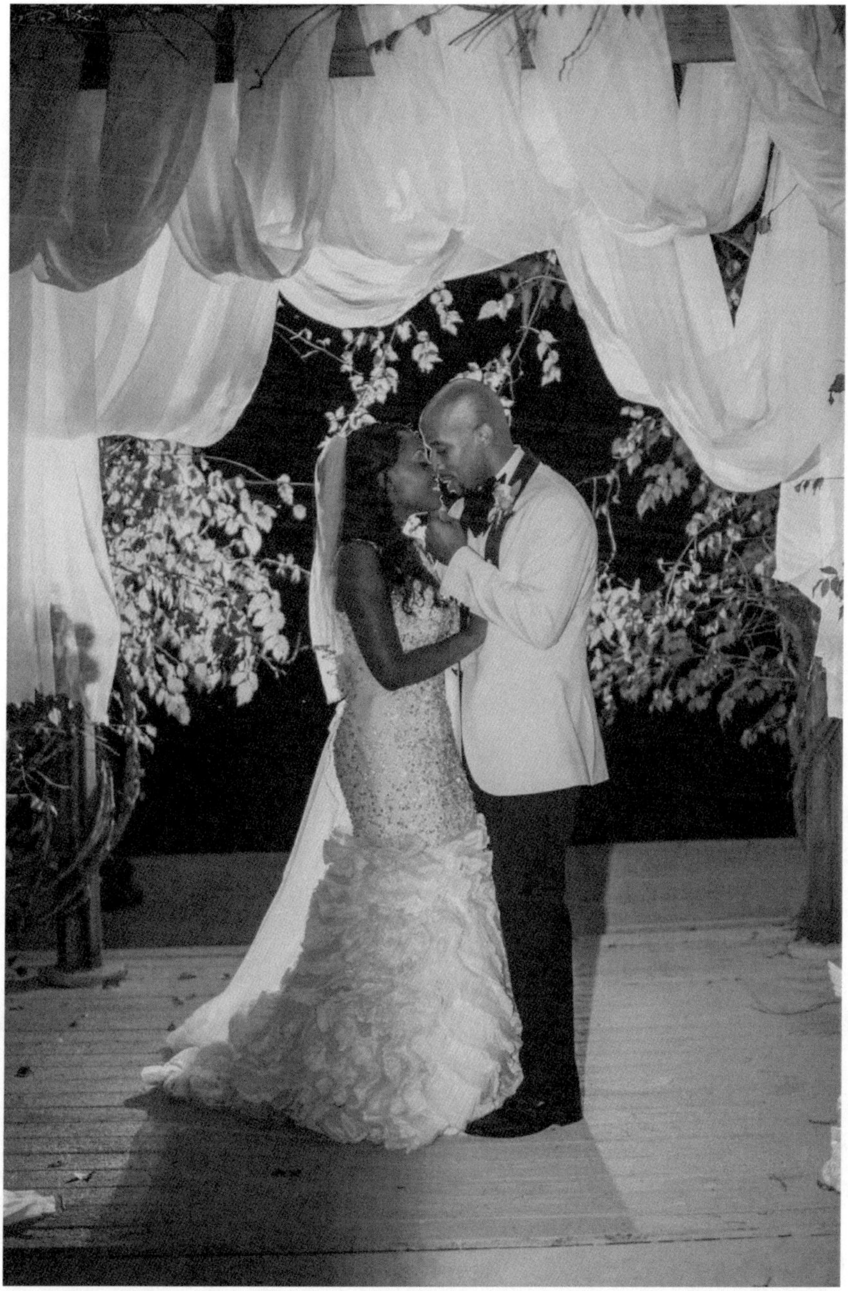

Today, we do not follow that as closely. It may seem insane, but there is a practical reason this was done. Looking at it from the gospel's point of view, while we are engaged to Christ, we are not able to physically be in His presence.

It is understood that because of sin, we lost the privilege of face to face communion with God. But, at the marriage of the lamb, for the first time we will have the intimacy of contact with our Lord and Savior.

The tradition of waiting until the wedding to even kiss is a symbol of what we are to experience with Christ. There will be no more restrictions between us and our savior. The longing desire that we have had, to be in his presence, will be fed.

THE ANNOUNCEMENT

After the kiss it is a standing tradition to announce the new name given to the bride. For example, in our case, before our marriage, we were Andrae B. Rickets and Lysbeth Jean-Louis. After our ceremonial kiss we were introduced to the world for the first time as Mr And Mrs. Andrae Ricketts. The custom is for the woman to take on a new name, the name of the husband given to him by His father.

So it is with Christ and His bride who, while standing on mount Sion with Him, will receive a new name, the name of His father. (Rev 14:1)

PRESENTS

When the wedding ceremony ends, there is a transition to the reception. Here the bridal party and guests partake of a massive feast together, celebrating the momentous occasion. At the reception, the guests have an opportunity to leave gifts for the newlyweds. Generally, the types of gifts received will be used in the kitchen and bathroom only. Common presents are pots, pans, plates, silverware, towels, and rags.

These are gifts that the groom would not be too excited about, but it means the world to the bride. It is safe to say that the majority, if not all, of the gifts will be given with the bride in mind. Yet there has yet to be a groom who feels slighted, because the bride is all the gift that he needs.

This is the same experience that Christ is to have with His bride as He is coming to the wedding bringing rewards with Him. "And, behold, I come quickly; and my reward is with me." (Revelation 22:12) The bride is to receive the gift of a transformed immortal body. (1Cor 15:51-53) Along with this, the bride will receive the gift of a crown. (2Tim 4:8) If that wasn't enough, the bride will also be taken back to paradise to dwell in mansions prepared for her. (John 14:1-3)

During this gift giving at the marriage of the Lamb, what gift will Christ receive? His bride is coming to Him empty handed. Even so, the greatest gift of all is the reception of the bride He waited so long for.

PARADISE

When the wedding is over, the bride will leave with the groom to go on their honeymoon. Usually, couples go to exotic places for this trip which can be summarized by one word, PARADISE.

When Jesus Christ takes His bride after the wedding, He will bring her to paradise. Knowing we are the bride, we can take comfort in this beautiful promise of being with Him in paradise. "He that hat an ear, let him hear what the Spirit saith unto the churches; To him that overcometh will I give to eat of the tree of Life, which is in the midst of the paradise of God." (Revelation 2:7)

FINAL THOUGHTS

We hope that you take much more than just how to find a mate from this book. We pray that you see an uplifted and crucified, yet risen savior. Our desire is for you to see how you need to allow Jesus into every facet of your life. If you heard His voice, answer the call and surrender to him today.

As you see how the gospel was applied to this area of your life, prayerfully search for other areas in your life this can be done to as well. Search for every aspect of your life to see if Jesus is present there. If you find places where He is absent, seek Him now while He may be found.

Jesus Christ told us that the Kingdom of God is with men. This means you can experience heaven on earth today, how bad do you want it? As we like to say:

"HEAVEN ON EARTH, IT'S A DECISION"

If you have further questions and would like to contact us, you can do so by going to our website: www.alttrinc.com.
You can also email us at alttrinc@gmail.com.
You can even call us at (662) 608-4057

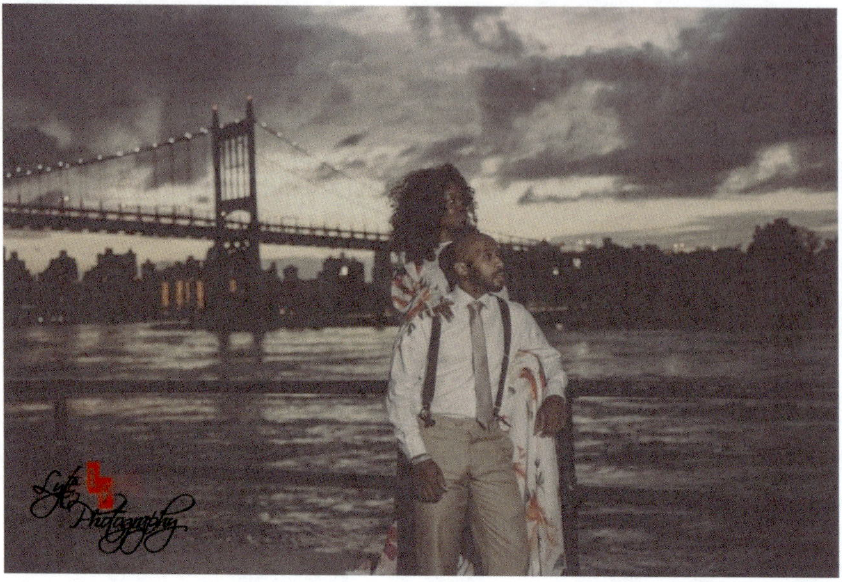

Made in the USA
Las Vegas, NV
10 November 2023